Satan's Lies

Overcoming the Devil's Attempts to Stunt Your Spiritual Growth

Michael W. Newman

To the people of Prince of Peace who hunger and thirst for righteousness;

To Cindy, evidence of Jesus' truth and love.

Contents

Satan's Lies
Your Outlook

Lie #1: "I Don't Really Exist"

A TRAVEL ODYSSEY

A few years ago a young man stopped by my office to give me an update about a trip he was going to take with his dad. This was going to be a very special trip. For years there was tension between the son and his father. But in recent years they had been working hard to get back on track. They were seeing counselors, evaluating the past, and taking a hard look at their own flaws and failures. Finally, they started to talk again. Issues were being addressed and resolved. There was some successful healing taking place. So, they decided to take another step in their growing and deepening bond together. They made a plan to get away for some father-son time. They booked a flight, packed their golf clubs, and headed to the airport. The son confided in me before the trip that this was going to be a very important time. He was planning to take some important steps in putting the past behind him, asking for a new beginning, and expressing his love to his dad.

When he stopped by my office to tell me about the trip, I was eager to hear how this crucial time together went. He said to me, "We never made it."

I was shocked! Never made it? "What happened?" I asked.

The young man told me a story of amazing complications and foul-ups. They got to the airport on time, but the plane was delayed. After the plane arrived and the passengers were boarded, a mechanical difficulty on the plane was discovered. Every passenger had to get off the plane, board a bus, and be transported to another waiting aircraft. My friend and his dad joined the rest of the passengers in this transportation odyssey. As the airline attendants checked the identification of each passenger boarding the new plane, the father reached for his wallet to get his ID. The wallet was gone! He realized that it must have fallen out of his pocket on the bus. The bus had already driven away, so an attendant asked an airline worker to call the driver and have someone check for the wallet. My friend and his dad waited. After half an hour, while already impatient passengers got even more impatient, the bus people called back. They couldn't find the wallet. That left my friend's dad with no money, no identification, and no ability to fly. Airline personnel retrieved their luggage, and father and son drove back home.

I couldn't believe it. All that progress in their relationship. All that preparation for a very meaningful trip— one that would serve as a marking point in life. All that for nothing. My first reaction was to say to the young man, "The devil really worked hard on that one. He didn't want you and your dad to take any steps to get closer."

I was a bit surprised at my friend's reaction. He said, "The devil? I never thought of that."

He told me that he just got aggravated at the endless hassles. "Typical travel craziness in Chicago," he said. He didn't connect it at all to an attempt by Satan to derail lives that were growing into a God-pleasing and God-glorifying relationship.

He didn't think about the spiritual battle that was taking place behind the scenes.

NOT JUST FLESH AND BLOOD

The Bible gives important information about what is really happening in our day to day lives. Ephesians 6:10-12 says:

> *"Finally, be strong in the Lord and in his mighty power. Put on the full armor of God so that you can take your stand against the devil's schemes. For our struggle is not against flesh and blood, but against the rulers, against the authorities, against the powers of this dark world and against the spiritual forces of evil in the heavenly realms."*

These verses contain important words from the Apostle Paul to people making their way through the very treacherous journey of life. He was letting them know that there is a lot more going on behind the scenes than meets the eye. It's not just ticket snafus and coincidental breakdowns. It's not just fluke temptations and typical aggravation. There is a spiritual battle raging every day.   And that spiritual battle directly impacts your life.

I want to be clear: I'm not advocating a "devil made me do it" attitude for every foul up, tragedy, or hurt that takes place in life. Our sinful flesh leads the way in wreaking plenty of havoc and doing loads of damage in life. But it is of critical importance that the truth of Ephesians chapter six is not overlooked. Our battle is not against flesh and blood. The powers of this dark world and the spiritual forces of evil in the heavenly realms are at work. And their goal is to foul up anything of God in your life. Their goal is to destroy you.

HOW IT ALL STARTED

Revelation chapter twelve gives an insightful summary of what Satan is up to. Verses one through eight open the chapter with a picture of the devil marshaling his forces in order to destroy the Savior Jesus who was about to be born. God's protective action intervened for the baby and mother.

Verse seven describes the heavenly warfare between Satan and his angels and Michael the archangel and his forces. Verse eight says that the devil *"was not strong enough, and they* (the evil angel allies) *lost their place in heaven."*

People wonder how Satan and his angels began their evil quest.   These verses give us the information.   More important, however, is the information these verses give us about three key truths of Satan's work: Satan's **activity**, his **attitude**, and his **aim**.

Verse nine makes his **activity** clear: *"The great dragon was hurled down—that ancient serpent called the devil, or Satan, who leads the whole world astray. He was hurled to the earth, and his angels with him."*

Satan leads the whole world astray. In John 8:44 Jesus described the devil's central activity: *"He was a murderer from the beginning, not holding to the truth, for there is no truth in him. When he lies, he speaks his native language, for he is a liar and the father of lies."*

Satan wants to deceive you in every way. Jesus said that lying is the devil's native language. This activity of lying, deception, promoting errant beliefs, spreading half-truths, and justifying wrongs brings a result that Satan delights in: separating you from a saving walk with Jesus. His lies, Jesus said, result in murder.

Back in Revelation twelve, verses 10-12 give the wonderful news that the devil was overcome. He would no longer be allowed to make his lying accusations about us before God. That was a major activity of Satan. He accused day and night. A great example of that is in Job chapter one. You may remember how the encounter between God and Satan went:

> *The LORD said to Satan, "Have you considered my servant Job? There is no one on earth like him; he is blameless and upright, a man who fears God and shuns evil."*

"Does Job fear God for nothing?" Satan replied. "Have you not put a hedge around him and his household and everything he has? You have blessed the work of his hands, so that his flocks and herds are spread throughout the land. But stretch out your hand and strike everything he has, and he will surely curse you to your face" (Job 1:8-11).

Accusations and a twisting of the truth were what Satan delighted in. But now, according to Revelation twelve, the blood of the Lamb and the word of testimony from believers overcame the devil's destructive attempts (more on that in just a bit). And because of that, the devil got ticked off!

The last part of verse twelve reveals Satan's **attitude**: *"But woe to the earth and the sea, because the devil has gone down to you! He is filled with fury, because he knows that his time is short."*

The devil is angry. He is "filled with fury." Literally, the Bible says the "devil was thrown down to you, having great rage." He tries to cover up his true colors. The devil tries to hide his hateful attitude. 2 Corinthians 11:14 says that *"Satan himself masquerades as an angel of light."* But that is only more deception. It is definitely a masquerade because Satan's attitude is anger, rage, and fury to the core. And that is what he wants to take out on you.

Verses 13-16 continue the warfare account of Revelation chapter twelve. These verses show that Satan's attention is turned toward the whole church—all believers. The woman that symbolized Mary in the beginning of the chapter now represents all who trusted Christ because of the child she bore. Verse 17 reveals Satan's **aim** as we wait for Christ to return: *"Then the dragon was enraged at the woman and went off to make war against the rest of her offspring--those who obey God's commandments and hold to the testimony of Jesus."*

If you believe in Jesus or are even contemplating a walk of faith, Satan has you as his target. He has declared war on your life. His aim is to take aim at you. That's the truth that 1 Peter 5:8 reinforces: *"Be self-controlled and alert. Your enemy the devil prowls around like a roaring lion looking for someone to devour."*

Sometimes Satan is portrayed as that little guy on people's shoulders who is just trying to convince everyone to loosen up and have some fun. "Why get so uptight?" some people claim. "The devil is just trying to give you a little excitement, a little action in your life."

Nothing could be further from the truth. A prowling and roaring lion is not looking for a party to go to. It's looking for prey to kill and devour. That is the devil's aim: to kill and devour any person he can ensnare. This is no game. It is life and death.

Satan's **activity**, **attitude**, and **aim** all add up to an attempt to work eternal hurt in the lives of every person on earth. His misery would love to have lots of company. His ways are senseless. They are chaotic. They're mean. Those are the devil's true colors!

IS ALL THIS MEANT TO SCARE YOU?

If you're getting frightened about all this, hold on. The danger of giving the devil too much attention is that he can get you to believe that he is an equal counterpart of God. That's another one of Satan's lies. The Bible says in 1 John 3:8, *"The reason the Son of God appeared was to destroy the devil's work."* That's what Jesus did when He died on the cross and rose from death. In fact, Satan's work has been exposed. 2 Corinthians 2:11 says, *"We are not unaware of [Satan's] schemes."*

The purpose of this book is to bring you the truth about some of the devil's lies so that you can be aware of what is really going on in your life, and with that awareness, as Ephesians chapter six said, *"You can take your stand against the devil's schemes."*

If anyone is shaking in his boots, it's the devil himself! Jesus said in John 3:20, *"Everyone who does evil hates the light, and will not come into the light for fear that his deeds will be exposed."* Whenever Satan and his schemes are dragged out into the light he trembles with fear. He doesn't want to face the Lamb of God. You might remember what happened when Jesus and Satan went one-on-one in the desert. In Luke chapter four (vss.1-13) Jesus repelled every attempt of the devil to thwart the Savior in His mission. Jesus spoke the authoritative Word of God and Satan ran!

The devil also doesn't want to hear the words of witness that overcame him. That's the good news that Revelation twelve gives. Satan has been defeated by the testimony of believers. The word for "overcame" in verse eleven of Revelation twelve literally means that the verdict was won. It paints a courtroom scene.

First, the blood of Jesus won the verdict. The indisputable evidence against any accusation Satan might level is the atoning blood of Jesus. All sins were covered by the blood of Christ. He took the punishment for all of us. Not one accusation can stand. As Jesus hung on the cross, God the Father ruled that His own Son was guilty of all our sin. For each one of us the Father declares the verdict that is filled with amazing grace: not guilty!

Second, the testimony of believers won the verdict over Satan. Literally verse eleven says, "The word of their public witness." Satan can't stand up to the out-loud testimony that reveals his lies and God's truth. Bring it all out into the light and the verdict is clear. The devil is done for.

This fact doesn't give us the right to get the Gatorade out and dump it on ourselves with pride in our victory. The fact is, we escape Satan's destructive efforts only by the grace of God. In his book <u>Between God and Satan</u> Helmut Thielicke points out that when it comes to confrontation with the devil, we can only rest in the strength of our Savior. He said, "We can only beg [God]: 'May the right man fight for us.' For we have no adequate weapon of our own, nor are we capable of wielding such a weapon; here we ourselves are the battleground."[1]

We are the turf that Satan wants to claim as his own. What an amazing and mind-boggling turn of events that God the Father sent the right man to fight for us. He loved us that much! He made us His own.

And that is exactly why we have no need to fear. We're not the ones fighting this cosmic battle. We follow the One who is fighting for us.

THE GREAT BRUSH-OFF

If this sounds like a bit too much to dig into, consider the words of C.S. Lewis in his work The Screwtape Letters. The senior devil, Screwtape, knew that any awareness of his schemes and existence would be a serious threat to success. So he advised his junior devil nephew, Wormwood, to keep his existence concealed:

> "I do not think you will have much difficulty in keeping the patient in the dark. The fact that 'devils' are predominantly comic figures in the modern imagination will help you. If any faint suspicion of your existence begins to arise in his mind, suggest to him a picture of something in red tights, and persuade him that since he cannot believe in that (it is an old textbook method of confusing them) he therefore cannot believe in you."[2]

Satan doesn't want you to believe that He exists. He doesn't want you on guard and ready. He doesn't want you praying for protection, wisdom, discernment, and clarity. He doesn't want you thinking, "Hey, these delays and these foul-ups for my trip may be Satan's way of trying to wreck the next step in my relationship with my dad."

My friend didn't think about spiritual warfare when his trip got ruined. After we talked, however, he took his dad out for lunch and had the talk he had first planned. Satan was steaming mad, but godly steps were taken in the relationship of this father and son.

As my friend and I talked that day in my office, we covered some basics in spiritual warfare. I read to him a quote from John Maxwell's book <u>Partners in Prayer</u>: "I believe the evil one watches for the right time to attack Christian leaders, and he is especially active before an advance for God's kingdom, after a victory, and when a leader is just plain tired."[3]

I shared with this young man that Satan's timing after some serious victories in his life was typical of the devil's method of operation. There are key times to watch out for Satan's attacks and this was one of them.

Satan continues his efforts to deceive. He will keep prowling around and whispering lies until Christ comes again. It's important to review some of his schemes so you can be ready. That's why this book will cover three key areas of your life into which Satan will try to inject his lies: Your outlook, your thoughts, and your actions. Each chapter will focus on one of Jesus' encounters with the demonic, with a Scriptural reference to the demonic activity around us, or with a hidden attack of Satan. My prayer is that you will grow in clarity, insight, and spiritual maturity as you watch our Lord and Savior reveal Satan's lies.

Chapter 1 notes:
[1]Thiekicke, Helmut. <u>Between God and Satan.</u> Grand Rapids, Michigan: Wm. B. Eerdmans Publishing Company, 1958, 27.
[2]Lewis, C.S. <u>The Screwtape Letters.</u> New York: MacMillen Publishing Company, 1982, 33.
[3]Maxwell, John. <u>Partners in Prayer.</u> Nashville: Thomas Nelson Publishers, 1996, 83.

Satan's Lies
Your Outlook

Lie #2: "Life is All Luck and Coincidence"

DO YOU BELIEVE IN LUCK?

Luke 4:13 says, *"When the devil had finished all this tempting, he left him until an opportune time."* An opportune time came very quickly. Luke 4:31-41 describes three episodes from Jesus' life. Each one of them involved a spiritual struggle. And each of those vignettes reveals a nuance of the lie that Satan tries to convince you is true, that **life is all luck and coincidence.**

Do you believe that? People talk about all kinds of luck—winning the lottery, meeting the right girl or guy, getting accepted into the right school, being at the right place at the right time to get that house or new job. Take a look at that envelope you just received in the mail. It says that you may have already won ten million dollars from the latest publishing house sweepstakes! Luck and coincidence. People talk about it all the time.

The Bible offers quite a contrast. God says in Jeremiah 29:11, *"For I know the plans I have for you, plans to prosper you and not to harm you, plans to give you hope and a future."* Plans! God never talks about your life being merely luck and coincidence. He always talks about your life and the lives of all His people in the context of a plan and of having purpose.

As you read, you may be thinking to yourself, "I know all this. I don't buy into the luck and coincidence lie."

Perhaps that's true on the outside. You may not use the word "luck" to address the way your life goes. You may be very open about the fact that God is doing His work and bringing His blessing to your life.

But Satan is very crafty. He may have already tricked you into living the lie that life is all luck and coincidence. How does He do it? Let's take a look at three ways the devil might lure you into the lie along with three ways Christ counteracts that lie for your life.

CHAOS VS. AUTHORITY

In Luke chapter four, verses 31-35 we hear that Jesus met a demon-possessed man in church. Luke described what happened: *"Then [Jesus] went down to Capernaum, a town in Galilee, and on the Sabbath began to teach the people. They were amazed at his teaching, because his message had authority. In the synagogue there was a man possessed by a demon, an evil spirit. He cried out at the top of his voice, 'Ha! What do you want with us, Jesus of Nazareth? Have you come to destroy us? I know who you are--the Holy One of God!'"*

Can you believe that? Right in the middle of church, as Jesus preached, an unclean demonic spirit shouted at Him. That would cause a stir in any church—and Satan loved every minute of its effects! The demon was in his element when he caused disruption in the synagogue because the devil and his allies thrive on confusion. God loves order, but Satan gets his thrills through chaos. In fact, he causes as much as he can. That's what was going on in the synagogue that day.

It is very important to grasp the true nature of Satan and sin. Chaos, injustice, disruption, and disorder are at the core of what it means to be apart from God. Almost everyone acknowledges that sin is wrong, that the devil tries to tempt you to do things that are against God's will, and that Satan does bad things. What people do not realize is that the devil thrives on chaos. He feeds on the nature of this corrupt and broken world. Accidents happen. Disasters wreak havoc on so many lives. The innocent die too soon. You may cry out to God and ask, "Where are you, God? Why are all these awful things happening? What is going on?"

And God weeps right along with you. He weeps with the people He loves so much. He is brokenhearted as He sees the corrupt and chaotic nature of life that is separated from him. It's the result of sin. Romans 8:22 lets us know that *"the whole creation has been groaning"* in brokenness, waiting to be restored by God. And God will restore us. He sent His Son to redeem us. He is reaching every person possible as we wait for His return. He is even keeping evil in check, not allowing it to proceed at full tilt (Rev. 20:1-3). For now, however, there is chaos. And Satan is smiling every time the chaotic nature of this broken world asserts itself. God is present to comfort, sustain, and give hope. Satan laughs with glee at the misfortune and disaster.

The devil also tries to convince you that chaos is normal. He tries to lead you into believing that life is a random and meaningless progression of events. Sometimes you're lucky. Sometimes you're not. A 6-year-old boy shoots a classmate in school. A van filled with college students crashes and several young people die. Someone you love is diagnosed with cancer.

At the same time you celebrate the birth of a baby. You enjoy your daughter's band concert. You go out with a friend for the evening. Good and bad. Lucky and unlucky.

Is life just a meaningless roll of the dice? Is chaos normal?

Sometimes it seems that way. Just watch the news on television or read the newspaper. Most of what you see is very bad. If that is a true representation of what is really happening in the world, then, Satan would argue, God either must be ignoring us or totally incapable of running the universe. Why trust a God like that?

Think about your experiences in life. If the ups and downs are just random movements of life that show how senseless everything is, then you may start to wonder whether or not YOUR life makes sense. You may wonder if YOUR life really matters. Maybe your being here is just a coincidence. All the while Satan is laughing with glee because he has just succeeded in devaluing God's creation and diluting God's purpose.

Do you see how it happens? This lie slowly seeps into your sense of worth and purpose. Listen to enough newscasts, get filled with all the terrible things going on, and soon you'll be thinking, "I can't make any difference in this world. I'm just a random speck on the face of the earth. Everything is spinning out of control. The overwhelming stream of bad news keeps coming. I might as well give up."

It's then that Satan claims victory. True, you don't believe in luck, but your life is being smothered by the lie that life is all luck and coincidence.

Fortunately, Jesus intervenes. He said to the chaotic demon in Luke 4: *"Be quiet! Come out of him!"* In fact, Jesus didn't just SAY that. He aggressively commanded and rebuked that spirit. Jesus did not take this lie of Satan lightly at all. Why? Because **chaos is a satanic cover-up of Christ's purpose for your life.**

Did you hear the word "authority" used two times in this episode from Jesus' life? The people were *"amazed at his teaching, because his message had authority" (vs.32).* And the people said, *"With authority and power he gives orders to evil spirits and they come out!" (vs.36)*

Authority. Chaos may rage for a while. It's happening in this broken and sinful world. But if your hopes and spirit are being, or have been, dashed by chaos, Jesus comes to you with

23

authority, the authority to expose the myth of meaningless luck and coincidence and to show you that **your life has purpose**. You are no accident. You are God's person, loved by Him, cherished by Him, unique and important to Him. You are here, not by chance, but for a reason. And no matter what chaos has assaulted you, God has plans for you. You are here because He needs you here. To any voice that would try to minimize that or take that away, Jesus says, "Be quiet!" In Luke chapter four Jesus counteracted chaos with His authority. One key question for your life is: Does your life have the authority of Jesus as the counterbalance to the lie of Satan?

If you drive around in Chicago during the winter, your car gets covered with a white salty residue from all the ice-melting salt spread on the roads. You can't even tell what color some cars are during the winter! What every driver looks forward to is that wonderful day when the temperature rises above freezing. That's the day when the car wash lines are long. Finally, the salt can be washed off the car! Finally, it's clean again.

If you go through life giving all your attention to the bad news of the world, the truth of God's presence and purpose are going to get covered up like a car caked with salt. You need to be washed off regularly. That's what the authoritative Word of God does. Ephesians 5:26 says that God's people are cleansed *"by the washing with water through the word."* Do you have the Word of God giving you a regular rinse in life? It's the authority we need.

Satan's lie tries to give you the outlook that life is up for grabs. But the authority of what God says and the redeeming work of Jesus quiet the noise of the chaotic world and put the exclamation point in the sentence: your life has purpose!

SUFFERING VS. DISCIPLESHIP

The next vignette from Luke four happened this way: *"Jesus left the synagogue and went to the home of Simon. Now Simon's mother-in-law was suffering from a high fever, and they asked Jesus to help her. So he bent over her and rebuked the fever, and it left her. She got up at once and began to wait on them"* (vss. 38-39).

A second way Satan will try to get you to buy into the lie that life is all luck and coincidence is through **suffering**. Suffering is hard. It drains you. Whether it is physical illness, mental illness, stress in relationships, or personal struggles, suffering can get you to lose hope.

How do you feel when you go through suffering? What do you think about? Do you feel like your life is totally sidetracked? That your life is on hold? Notice that when Jesus encountered suffering in Luke 4, He rebuked it. In the same way He rebuked and commanded the spirit in verse 35, Jesus commanded the fever to go away. Jesus demonstrated that the demonic was at the root of this suffering. In fact, Jesus' action shows us an important principle: **suffering can be used by Satan to cover-up the strategic position you have as a worker in God's kingdom.**

Did you notice what the fever was preventing Simon's mother-in-law from doing? Serving Jesus! The word in this reading for "waited on them" actually is the word for Christian service. It's the word we get "deacon" or "deaconess" from. It's the word Jesus used when He said *"The Son of Man came to serve and to give His life as a ransom for many"* (Mark 10:45). Suffering was disrupting discipleship! So Jesus drove it out and He shows you that every moment of your life is one of important service to Him. **Your life has a strategic position in His kingdom.**

My friend Mary was in her 90's. She had one leg amputated. Her family home in the country was sold and she lived in a nursing home. But God's Word and Christ's presence kept lifting up that shroud of suffering to show Mary that she had a strategic position in God's kingdom. And you should have seen how she was Christ's shining light in that nursing home! She showed love to the nurses and aides. She encouraged fellow residents and helped organize a Bible study during the week. She spoke about her faith in Jesus to young people who made visits to the residents. Mary even mentored a young girl who became a regular visitor. This young girl ended up devoting her life to missionary work. Mary was in a strategic place to make a difference for the kingdom of God.

It's not always in a feel-good kind of way, but Jesus brings life even into suffering and death. My friend Mary was serving for the kingdom. Her suffering was under Jesus' command, and lives were being reached.

Maybe you are suffering right now. Maybe you feel lousy. You're worried. You're stressed and dissatisfied. You are bearing the burden of illness. Is it bad luck? Is your life on hold? Don't believe it! **Your life has a strategic position in God's kingdom** today! Suffering does not dilute your service for God's kingdom. Sometimes it steps it up a few notches. Sometimes you grow from it. Sometimes it sends you into situations that you would have never been in before—so you can reach people you would have never reached!

And even if suffering ends your life, Jesus promises that you will still serve Him on high forever. Satan wants you to believe that suffering puts you in the unlucky position of being useless in the world. Jesus lifts the shroud of suffering and shows you that, because of His love for you, **your life has a strategic position in God's kingdom** even in the midst of (and, perhaps because of) your suffering!

FEAR VS. LOVE

The final episode in this section of Luke exposes another tool of Satan: *"When the sun was setting, the people brought to Jesus all who had various kinds of sickness, and laying his hands on each one, he healed them. Moreover, demons came out of many people, shouting, 'You are the Son of God!' But he rebuked them and would not allow them to speak, because they knew he was the Christ" (4:40-41).*

A third way Satan will try to get you to buy into the lie that life is all luck and coincidence is through **fear**. The demons were shouting, "You are the Son of God!" They were scared and were shouting news that Jesus wanted to reveal at His pace and at the pace of God the Father. So Jesus commanded the demons into silence.

Fear needs everything right now. Fear says, "You may never have another chance. What if the future isn't what you want it to be? What if you don't meet that person who is right for you? What if you don't make the team? What if you don't have kids? What if your schedule isn't the way you planned? What if everything isn't happening for you right now?!" Fear drives you to control. You take the burden of the future on your shoulders.

Have you tried to carry that burden before? It's a heavy one isn't it? Fear says that you are alone in this life of chance, and you may be the only resource available to make it all work. **Fear can be used by Satan to cover-up the fact that your life is precious to God.** Satan wants to conceal the fact that God can be trusted to unfold the events of your life in just the right way and at just the right time. If you end up trusting God with your life, you just may trust Him with your eternity. Satan does not want that to happen.

Jesus steps in to counteract fear with His love. In Luke four, Jesus compassionately laid His hands on each person who came to Him. He took time and showed amazing love. Do you think Jesus will give you any less attention?

Maybe you feel like your life is in disarray and filled with uncertainty. You may look at the pile on your dining room table, or inside that storage room that you've been neglecting, or even at some serious issues in your life, and wonder. But Satan is lying. Your life is not merely disarray and uncertainty. It is not just luck and coincidence. You see, Jesus Christ fought for your life in an intentional and purposeful way when He gave His life on the cross. When Jesus battled sin and death and the devil, and then stood in victory at the resurrection, He showed the importance of your life. He made it clear that **your life is precious to God**.

Jesus said, *"Peace I leave with you; my peace I give you. I do not give to you as the world gives. Do not let your hearts be troubled and do not be afraid."* He replaces fear with His love for you. Paul exposes the source of fear in 2 Timothy 1:7, *"For God did not give us a spirit of timidity, but a spirit of power, of love and of self-discipline."*

Today Jesus Christ fights for you. Every moment—future included—is in the realm of His love and forgiveness. The Bible says in 1 John 4, *"Perfect love drives out fear" (vs.18).* That is how Christ counteracts fear and the lie that luck is all that carries you into the future. **Your life is precious to God!**

WHAT DO YOU BELIEVE ABOUT YOUR LIFE?

Will you fall for the lie that life is all luck and coincidence? Not if Christ can help it! His Word of authority counteracts chaos. His discipleship purpose for your life brings light and hope into your suffering. His love drives out fear as you rejoice in the fact that your life—however it may be going—is precious to God.

Is this good news for you? Do you need to hear the life-restoring and outlook changing Word of God? If this is what you need, I can tell you one thing for sure: today is not your lucky day.

It's much more than that!

Satan's Lies
Your Outlook

Lie #3: "Life is Supposed to Get Easier"

LIFE IS HARD

I was at Toys R Us one day looking at toys. As I scanned the shelves filled with items, I saw a toy called the "Momma Bear." It is a soft cuddly bear designed to go into a newborn baby's crib. With the flip of a switch the bear makes the sounds that the baby would hear while it was in the mother's womb— these are actual recorded sounds, the label says! It's supposed to be soothing to a baby.

You realize, don't you, that this "Momma Bear" was designed under the premise that life is hard—even for babies? When they are born they go through quite a transition, don't they? One minute cuddly and warm, the next minute not a lot of pleasant things going on! Maybe the "Momma Bear" could help them out.

Life is hard. You know it.
Diaper rash, skinned knees and bumped heads.
Falling off the bike, out of the tree and down the stairs.
The first day of school.
The last day of school.
Multiplication tables!

Science projects!
Hurt feelings.
Driver's Education.
Gym class.
The first traffic ticket.
A dented car.
A broken heart.
ACT's, SAT's.
Tuition.
Relationships.
No job.
Job!
Responsibilities!
Family conflict.
Loneliness.
Aches and pains.
Grief.
Illness.
Worry.
Retirement?
The golden years?
A rough world for grandchildren.
Uncertain health.
One day, death.
Life is hard.

Now, I'm not trying to be a wet blanket. I'm not trying to get you depressed. I'm not saying that there is no joy in life. God pours out joy and blessing into our lives. But there is plenty of hardship in this broken world of ours. The fall into sin set a pace of pain and sweat. I have not met a person in any generation from infancy to old age who has not experienced the rigors of life that can be very hard.

EASE, PLEASE

If you want to know the truth, nobody likes that very much. If the Gallup organization conducted a public opinion survey that asked the question, "Would you like life to become easier or more difficult over the next ten years? Circle your preference below," I'm pretty sure the response would lean strongly to the easier side. You and I want life to be a little easier on us. Hard times should be in the past. Good days, more prosperous days, more satisfying days, should lie ahead. We want to get richer, stronger, more tanned, more popular, more influential, and more happy. We want progress. Life should get easier.

That desire may not send you running to the store to buy a "Momma Bear." But Microwaves, remote controls, air-conditioning, and the word processing program I am using to write this book all say, "Let's make life a little easier." That's the way we are.

It's not surprising, then, that Peter leaned toward the easier side of life in Mark chapter eight. Jesus said to His disciples in verses 30-31, "Don't talk about me being the Messiah." Then He began to teach boldly and openly that *"the Son of Man must suffer many things and be rejected by the elders, chief priests and teachers of the law, and that he must be killed and after three days rise again;"*

That's when Peter rebuked Jesus. Those words of Jesus were hard to hear. Peter wanted life to be easier now that the Messiah, the Christ, was there. It was supposed to be political gain and social easy street. Peter didn't want suffering. He wanted life to be easier.

That's a very real tension that exists in your life today. You watch TV and realize that your special moments do not occur with a music soundtrack playing softly behind them. You don't experience the great times in slow motion. You can't always preserve the "Kodak moments." You don't drive your car on a closed course with a professional driver; you're lined up bumper to bumper on a congested expressway. Good times go by quickly. Life is fleeting. When you look in the mirror you don't see a retouched photo from a fashion magazine. All of your problems don't get resolved in a thirty or sixty minute episode. But there are times you wish they did. You do want life to be easier.

BETWEEN GOD AND SATAN

Let's remember what Jesus said about all this. He was very clear: *"In this world you will have trouble"* (John 16:33). *"I am sending you out like sheep among wolves"* (Matthew 10:16). The Bible also chimes in: *"Man is born to trouble as surely as sparks fly upward"* (Job 5:7). *"The length of our days is seventy years--or eighty, if we have the strength; yet their span is but* trouble and sorrow, for they quickly pass, and we fly away" _(Psalm 90:10)._

But Satan has a lie for you. He says, **"Life is supposed to get easier."** That's what he presented to Adam and Eve in the Garden of Eden. He said, "Go ahead and eat that fruit. Disobey God's plan. If you do, _"you will be like God, knowing good and evil" (Genesis 3:5)._ "Life is supposed to get easier," Satan lies.

When Jesus was tempted in the wilderness, Satan lured Him with an easier life—stones into bread, evading hardship, getting wealth. "Life is supposed to get easier," Satan lied to Jesus.

This lie plays with your emotions and energy levels. If life doesn't get easier, then is God disappointing you? Is He abandoning you? As life that is broken by sin keeps moving ahead and is hard, Satan whispers in your ear, "Maybe God isn't faithful. Maybe life isn't worth living. Suffering shouldn't happen. It can result in nothing good."

If you really believe that life is supposed to get easier, you may end up living in bitterness and disillusionment, guilt and anger, disappointed with God and pushing Him away. And that's exactly the way the devil wants your life to be.

THE REAL DEAL

So what is the real course of life? It was described well by a great artist, a world-renowned painter, who was planning a visit to a local high school art class. The students prepared for his visit by doing some of their own artwork. They did drawings and watercolor work. Some even tried oils. They had fun preparing. Some students groaned about the extra work, others had fun getting ready, and there were a number of students who worked very hard on their artwork during the class preparation. Finally, the day arrived for the artist to visit. He gave a talk to all the art students about his experiences and career. He was on a panel of judges for a school art exhibit. And at the end of the day there was an opportunity for a question and answer time with the artist. It took a little while for the students to get comfortable in dialog, but slowly they loosened up. That's when one boy raised his hand and asked, "When will my paintings bring in as much money as yours?" The class members snickered and the artist smiled. He knew the question would come up some time. He looked at the boy and said, "Your paintings may be valuable one day. You just need to do two things. Put your life into creating them, and then, die. Money may come in at that point."

The student wanted the easy way. The artist spoke the truth that the most meaningful course in life is a way of sacrifice that leads to value.

THE WAY OF VALUE

You are God's painting. God put His life into making you a new creation. The blood of Christ was placed on the canvass of your life, not to make life easy—a quick work whipped up in a couple of art classes, but to give you priceless value. God did not design your life to be one that slowly phases out of any difficulty and challenge and slides gradually into a life of leisure and complete ease. He called you by name, made you His own through Jesus, and set you apart as an invaluable servant in His kingdom.

Jesus said in Mark 8:31, *"The Son of Man must suffer many things and be rejected by the elders, chief priests and teachers of the law…he must be killed and after three days rise again."*

Life didn't get easier for Jesus. But because of His hard suffering, His death, and His resurrection for you, He accomplished the most worthwhile feat in history. He rescued humanity from destruction. He made your life a priceless work of art.

The real course of life is not the way of ease, but **the way of sacrifice that brings value**. The first facet of this way of value shows that **your life is valued by God Himself**. Jesus said to Peter in Mark 8:33, *"Get behind me, Satan!"* This wasn't Jesus saying, "Get out of my face." He wasn't telling Peter to leave the group of disciples. "Get behind me" means "follow me." It means, "Get in step with the way I am leading." Jesus was making it very clear that your life is not meant to be a snooze by the roadside. Your life is meant to be one that traces the steps of your Savior who leads the way. He leads the way through suffering, sin, and death. He leads the way in serving others. He leads the way to heaven. He leads the way in living life with sacrifice that brings value.

Jesus wants you included in that life, and He went to great lengths to get you there. In baptism you're put behind Jesus. He is in front as your strength and shield. Through communion, the presence of Jesus Christ, you are plopped behind Jesus again. He is in front as your Redeemer and Hope. God's Word shepherds you behind Jesus again. He is your Savior and Leader. Jesus' sacrifice brings you into a life that is valued.

True, life gets hard, but God works hard for your life. That is what the Bible says. Psalm 46:1 says, *"God is our refuge and strength, an ever-present help in trouble."* A refrain in Psalm 107 repeats four times, *"They cried out to the LORD in their trouble, and he delivered them from their distress."* The prophet Nahum in the Old Testament said, *"The Lord is good, a refuge in times of trouble. He cares for those who trust in him"* *(1:7)*. In John 16 Jesus said, *"In this world you will have trouble."* But Jesus added, *"But take heart! I have overcome the world"* *(vs.33)*. Your life is valued by God.

The second facet of this way of value shows that your life will bring value to others. Jesus talked about the calling for your life in Mark chapter 8: *"Then he called the crowd to him along with his disciples and said: 'If anyone would come after me, he must deny himself and take up his cross and follow me. For whoever wants to save his life will lose it, but whoever loses his life for me and for the gospel will save it'"* *(Mark 8:34-35)*. Real value in life, real gain and meaning, come from getting behind Jesus and doing the hard work of sacrificing yourself so others can know Him, know His love, and be saved.

In a visit to a nursing home I had the privilege of meeting Otto and Gretchen. They were married for 67 years. Gretchen, the love of Otto's life, couldn't communicate with him anymore. She was confined to a wheelchair. Three years ago Otto decided that Gretchen needed to enter a nursing home. But she wasn't going alone. Otto sold his house, got rid of their possessions, and moved into the nursing home with her. His beloved Gretchen wasn't going to be alone. That wasn't an easy decision. But loving sacrifice brought value to a precious bride. That is Jesus' way.

I'll never forget the time a mom and dad I know were faced with the difficult task of seeing their daughter through brain surgery: all the preparation, the tests, the arrangements, and, finally, the surgery. The parents did all they could do for her. They waited and they prayed. It wasn't easy. It wasn't included in the "Congratulations on Your Baby Daughter" owner's manual. But it was loving sacrifice that brought value to a little girl's life. That is Jesus' way.

Jesus told the apostle Peter in John chapter 21, *"I tell you the truth, when you were younger you dressed yourself and went where you wanted; but when you are old you will stretch out your hands, and someone else will dress you and lead you where you do not want to go" (vs.18).* In his book <u>In the Name of Jesus</u> Henri Nouwen used this verse to illustrate the way of suffering and sacrifice in the life of one who follows Jesus.[1] Jesus was letting Peter know that he would die for the Gospel.

The truth is that all of us, as we are placed behind Jesus, will be led to places that we may not want to go. Life will be hard. You may not feel like tackling the challenges before you. But as you follow Jesus, you walk in the way of sacrifice that brings value—the value of God's love and purpose—to the people God has placed in your life.

Over and over again I have seen that the most difficult challenges of life may be saved for later in life. As you get older, as you experience more, as your faith matures (it's supposed to!), God saves some very big and demanding jobs: health issues, radical life change, the rigors of parenting, the complexity of ethical challenges. The reality is that life will get more and more difficult. It is in that difficulty that you will have the greatest opportunities to make a difference for God's kingdom. Satan will try to convince you that a more difficult life is a disappointing life. God lets you know that He is simply entrusting you with more of His very important work. As Jesus said, *"From everyone who has been given much, much will be demanded; and from the one who has been entrusted with much, much more will be asked" (Luke 12:48).*

How can you keep going as life brings more challenge? Jesus gave the answer. He said, "Get behind me." He will bring you through. He will give you a life that is truly valuable.

It's natural for us to hope that there will be some ease in life. And God is gracious. He gives us rest and replenishment along the way. But what an amazing gift we have received from

God in the most certain hope of all: every day, by His grace, life can be lived the way it's supposed to be. Behind Jesus.

Chapter 3 notes:
[1]Nouwen, Henri J.M. <u>In the Name of Jesus.</u> New York: Crossroad Publishing, 1994, 61-62.

Satan's Lies

Your Outlook

Lie #4: "Some People Are Beyond God's Grace"

_____

AN AMAZING ENCOUNTER

In John chapter nine, an amazing encounter happens. Jesus comes face to face with a person we might describe as a "loser." Verse one says, *"As [Jesus] went along, he saw a man blind from birth."* Blind, begging, homeless, sitting at the side of the road. He was dirty. He was helpless. People thought he was a nuisance.

But Jesus brought a new dimension to this experience. When the disciples pressed Jesus about how this man's life got so fouled up, Jesus revealed a glimpse of how God looks at us:

> *"His disciples asked him, 'Rabbi, who sinned, this man or his parents, that he was born blind?'*
>
> *'Neither this man nor his parents sinned,' said Jesus, 'but this happened so that the work of God might be displayed in his life'"* (vss.9:1-3).

What work of God? What was Jesus talking about?

He was talking about grace.

Jesus knew the whole story about this blind beggar. What if we knew it, too? What if it went something like this...

THE STORY OF JOHN CHAPTER NINE

A long time ago in the region of Palestine, in the city of Jerusalem, the cry of a baby was heard shattering the quietness of the early morning hours. This was not an uncommon event— just as it is not an uncommon event for any bloodshot-eyed, exhausted parent reading these words. But to his parents, this newborn son might as well have been the center of the universe. He was their firstborn. After nine long months, their heart's desire had arrived. They named him John.

John's father was a blacksmith. The minute he heard the cries and rushed in to see the baby, the instant the midwives told him, "It's a boy," Daddy imagined working side by side with his son. With a skilled hand, a strong arm and a sharp eye, he would help the family prosper. And they would have the joy of being together. What a family this would be! What a mark they would make on the city of Jerusalem!

But soon those hopes and dreams were shattered. You see, very soon John's parents realized that he couldn't see them. He couldn't see anything. He didn't focus on his mother's face when she nursed him. He didn't follow his daddy's hand as he played with him. John was blind.

Today there would be schools and programs, education and sports, medical advances and the latest technology to give John a good life. But then, in first century Jerusalem, what could John's parents hope for? A physical defect was seen as a consequence of a personal misdeed. No one was reaching out with help and understanding. The family was shunned. The business was avoided. They couldn't even bring John to worship. Life crumbled around them.

John grew. His parents loved him. They took care of him. They eked out a living to provide for his needs. But for John there was no real hope. He felt the brokenness and hurt of this sinful world firsthand. John grew up and became a beggar. Cut off from church, family, and community, he had an awful life. There he sat in Jerusalem. No one even knew his name. He was just the beggar who was born blind.

THE OUTCAST

John was an outcast. To the disciples that day, the blind man was a hopeless cause. "He must have been suffering the result of a terrible misdeed," they thought. "Let's ask Jesus about the cause, but not about the possibility of help. There is no help for this guy."

Before you shake your head in disgust at the disciples' assumption, think about how you may have made the same assumption about people you've run across. Maybe they were avowed atheists. Maybe they were hardened criminals. Maybe they were drugged out rock stars or people immersed in promiscuous sexual behavior. "Hopeless," you may have thought.

People thought the same thing about Matthew the tax collector. People thought the same thing about Saul, who later became Paul. In fact, people didn't think highly of any of the disciples. Their group included lowly fishermen, political outcasts, young whippersnappers and once-corrupt businessmen.

Isn't it amazing? These are the people we would consider lost causes, undependable, too extreme, immoral— even dangerous! But Jesus reached these people. He showed the fabric of God's character: Grace. Not one of them was beyond God's grace.

Satan wants to cover up that fact. He desperately shouts, "It can't be true! God's grace can't be for you! You're too corrupt. You're too far gone. You've failed too many times."

Satan points out all the people who seem so much better than you. They look good. They have nice things. Their houses are neat and clean. They are involved in so many community activities. "Maybe they are cut out for God's grace, but not you!" Satan says.

Unfortunately, Satan doesn't understand God's grace. In Philip Yancey's book, <u>What's So Amazing About Grace?,</u> he told the story of his friend Mel. Mel suffered because of his struggle with homosexuality. Yancey describes a dialog that took place between a TV interviewer and Mel's parents. The interviewer asked, "You know what other Christians are saying about your son. They say he's an abomination. What do you think about that?"

Mel's mother replied in a tender and loving way, "Well, he may be an abomination, but he's still our pride and joy."

Yancey summarized a nuance of grace: "In some ways we are all abominations to God...and yet somehow, against all reason, God loves us anyhow. Grace declares that we are still God's pride and joy."[1]

Like Mel and the blind man in John chapter nine, we can find ourselves getting berated, browbeaten and abused. People can be downright unkind. Your talents can be minimized, your self-worth can be demolished, and your sense of value can be squashed.

On the other hand, you can do the same to other people. You can view others as worthless, too far gone, unreachable, and undesirable.

That is exactly the half-truth that Satan wants to perpetuate. You? You are beyond God's grace. Other people? They're beyond God's grace. The evidence of failure, inadequacy, and unworthiness is plentiful. How could God love any of us? Why would He want to love you? Why would He want to love all those other people who are so odd and annoying?

That's a half-truth. Satan is right that we're unworthy. Satan is correct in his assessment of our failure and inadequacy.

God even lets us know in His Word that *"there is no one righteous, not even one" (Romans 3:10).* A few verses later Paul declares: *"All have sinned and fall short of the glory of God" (Romans 3:23).* Yes, we don't deserve God's love. No one does! But Satan leaves out the other half of the truth: we're still God's pride and joy! You are not beyond God's grace. The people around you are not beyond God's grace. God's grace is exactly what we need, and it is precisely what God supplies.

When Jesus answered the disciples in John nine, He revealed the amazing characteristic of God's grace. There was a story behind the story of the blind man. As Paul Harvey says, let's consider "the rest of the story."

THE STORY BEHIND THE STORY

The misery, rejection and suffering weren't the only things going on in John's life. There was another story too. A long time before John sat in the dusty streets begging, a long time before John even was born, there was conversation in heaven. God the Father sat with His Son as they discussed an amazing occurrence, a demonstration of God's grace. God reviewed the list of what he wanted His Son to do.

"You'll be doing a lot of healing," the Father said to His Son. "One specific assignment I want to give you concerns a blind beggar in Jerusalem named John. When you're there, find him. He'll have no way of knowing you, but find him. Do this work before you leave. Find him and heal him. He has been suffering for a long time. I care about him so much and I want him to know me. Make it clear that you are the one who healed his blindness. And show him that his life doesn't merely involve making a mark on Jerusalem like his father hoped; his life will make a mark on the world. Many people will see because of John."

The Son replied, "Why don't I spit on the ground and make some mud to smear on his eyes. He can't see, but he can hear and feel. He'll hear me spit, and he'll feel that mud. Then I'll tell him to wash in the pool that is formed from the spring flowing from Temple hill. They call it Siloam. That will show him that blessings do flow from you, Father, and from the One you have sent."

The Father chimed in, "Excellent plan! Why don't you do this on the Sabbath? It's supposed to be a day when people look to me, but it's become a day when my people look to themselves and their rules."

That day in heaven, the plan was made. It was designed for John, just for him. One person, one life, recorded forever in the assignment book of the Son of God. John was not beyond God's grace. His life was meant for it. He was God's pride and joy.

JOHN NINE CONTINUED...

So Jesus did His work while it was day. The Light of the world shined for the blind beggar. John heard the spit. He felt the mud. He heard the command, *"Go wash in the pool of*

49

Siloam." He did it, and he saw! He saw! For the first time ever, he saw!

What did he see? Neighbors who didn't believe it was him. He told them his story. They still didn't believe him! The community that shunned him was a major disappointment. So what did he get to see next? Church! For the first time ever John stood with the Pharisees, the leaders of worship and the life of faith. For the first time John felt that he could be close to God. But the Pharisees didn't believe him! They scolded him. They dragged his parents in and put them under more pressure and scrutiny. When he was blind he thought church would be a sanctuary. But John realized that something was missing. It was strange. He felt closer to God when that man called Jesus spit, put mud on his eyes, and told him to go wash. So John told the Pharisees. He told them that they were disciples of the wrong thing. He told them that only God could have healed him because a blind beggar was an outcast. He had no hope. He deserved no favor. From the beginning of time no one had ever healed a blind man. John told the group that he must have met God!

Then what did John see? He saw the door. Then he saw the street. Those Pharisees threw him out.

FEELING UNDESERVING

Perhaps you've felt like the once-blind man when the church leaders threw him into the street: undeserving, alone, unwanted. There may be times when you are very conscious of your own imperfection. Your self-confidence may be at a low ebb. Deep inside you may feel like you never can do well enough.

When I was growing up, my parent's marriage deteriorated slowly over the years. Finally, when I was in college, they divorced. Over the years, as I spoke with children whose parents divorced, I found that a common thread among many of them was an ingrained lack of confidence. I could relate to the feeling. If something was going wrong, my first thought would be, "How am I fouling this up?" If I experienced some dissonance in a relationship I would immediately believe that the whole thing was going to self-destruct. The relationship was in danger of ending. I spoke with many other people who experienced the same gut-reaction of doubt and hopelessness. No matter how many compliments came our way, the prevailing feeling of insecurity seemed to dominate.

Part of my journey out of this shadow of doubt was having conversations with people who grew up in secure homes. A friend of mine mentioned that his first thought in approaching a new venture or challenge has always been, "I can do this. Why not give it a try?" Doubt and uncertainty weren't part of his life growing up. He just forged ahead. My wife's confidence in our relationship has played a big part in my changed outlook. Whenever we experienced friction in our marriage, she would never even consider that things were going to crumble. Her life was built on confidence, not instability.

Another key component in fighting prevailing doubt and low confidence has been God's grace in my life. Satan wants to tie me down to my past. He wants my life to be built on instability. But God says, "You're my pride and joy." Philip Yancey said, "Grace means there is nothing we can do to make God love us more...And grace means there is nothing we can do to make God love us less."[2] Our lives are built on the bedrock of God's love.

Satan does not want you to know that. He'll let you know that you're a sinner, that you can't be perfect, that nothing you do is ever enough, but he will never whisper a word about God's grace. He'll tell you that you're too far gone. He'll try to convince you that you could never ever repent, that you could never ever have a new beginning or another chance. He will try to convince you that your imperfection is a barrier to God's reach into your life. But he will never let you know that God's grace is designed with our imperfection in mind! When we're face-down in the dirt, Jesus picks us up and says, "You're right. You can't do well enough on your own. But I'm here to fill in the gaps. I'm here to be perfect in your place. I'm here to give you a gift—you're God's pride and joy anyway!"

God sees you when you are laying in the dust, drained, empty and hopeless. He saw John after he was thrown out by the Pharisees, too.

MEANWHILE...

This face-down in the dirt position was not an unforeseen development as God the Father sat with His Son in heaven's strategy room.

"His life will get a lot harder," the Father said. "You'll have to find him again. Make sure that I don't lose John."

The Son said, "I'll track him down. I'll do everything I can to bring Him to you."

So there he was, face covered with dust, squinting with debris in his newly seeing eyes. Jesus approached him and said, "Do you believe in the Son of Man?"

John knew what he didn't want to believe in— harshness, lovelessness, meanness and no acceptance. He just got a major dose of that. So John replied, "Who is he, sir? Tell me, so that I may believe in him."

And Jesus felt His Father smile with delight. The Son, the One Sent to remove blindness, said to John, "You have now SEEN him; in fact, he is the one speaking with you."

John fell on his face, held onto Jesus' ankles and said, "Yes, Lord, I believe!" And there in the street, his hair and face and clothes covered with dust, John knew that God had come for him, for him! His tears of joy mixed with the dust on his face as he worshipped for the very first time.

Jesus let John see. John saw through the dust and dirt. He saw through the lie of Satan. He saw that He was not beyond God's grace. He saw that God's grace was meant for him.

Jesus did the impossible. Hope for a blind and hopeless beggar? That was impossible. But that's God's business—to reach the unreachable, to change the unchangeable, to save the unsaveable, to do the impossible.

When Jesus told the disciples that even a rich person, a person who has his life together, a person with every benefit and blessing, a polished and articulate and educated person, would have a very difficult time getting into heaven, they replied, "Who then can be saved?"

Jesus answered, *"With man this is impossible, but with God all things are possible"* (Matthew 19:24-26).

Do you feel unreachable? Jesus is tracking you down. Do you see someone who looks like a lost cause? Jesus is tracking that person down. He may even use you to help. No matter what the devil says, no one is beyond God's grace. That's what John saw. And he saw a lot more as the days went by...

WHAT JOHN SAW

When John heard Jesus call the Pharisees blind, he realized that he would be seeing things they would be missing.

What did John see as his life went on in that long ago time in the land of Palestine?

He saw Jesus in action. John wasn't going to stray far from God. He would have held onto His ankles forever on that Jerusalem street if he could. But there were more assignments for Jesus on this earth. John saw Him suffer. John saw the blood drip into His eyes from the crown of thorns. He saw Jesus wince as the slivers from the cross dug into his beaten back. John saw Jesus cry out, "Father, forgive them!" and "It is finished!" He saw Jesus do something remarkable. The One who could heal a man born blind didn't have to suffer and die. John knew that. But Jesus' completion of this assignment was rooted in the same motivation for completion of John's healing—God's grace. All John could think as he watched Jesus die was, "He must be carrying a lot of people just like me in His heart." John was right. This was amazing—amazing grace!

It was just as another John wrote centuries later—John Newton, the former slave trader,

> "Amazing grace, how sweet the sound
> That saved a wretch like me.
> I once was lost, but now am found,
> Was blind, but now I see."

And the once-blind John in Jerusalem kept seeing. The events that followed seemed like a blur. The tomb didn't hold Jesus. John's Savior was alive! He saw it with his own eyes. As time passed, John pondered these things when he gathered and prayed with fellow believers. He saw many lives changed and many wonders accomplished.

And one day, as an old man, with faithful friends around him, John lay on his deathbed. His bright eyes closed. His earthly days of seeing ended. But there was another surprise in store.

John kept seeing! In heaven, he looked around with awe. He was with Jesus again! It was better than holding on to His ankles on that dusty road! John, who had developed the habit of being close to Jesus during his life, did the same in heaven. One day he happened to run across the Father and the Son in heaven's strategy room. They talked and planned. John just looked around. He saw books in alphabetical order. He pulled one out from the letter "P" section. "Palestine." There was his name. There was God's plan to reach his small life. The will of God for one person. Amazing grace. Everywhere he looked he saw amazing plans. Encounters with Jesus through baptism and communion and friends and neighbors and worship! Personal encounters with Jesus that healed and restored and gave hope and direction! The Savior overcoming sin, overcoming blindness!

"So many ways of reaching!" John thought. So many names that he didn't know. But so many people precious to God. And there before him, plans. There before him, God's will of help and salvation for each one person. There before him, the expansive and wonderful grace of God.

John looked over his shoulder and glanced back at the Father and the Son as they worked and planned together. He strained to hear what they were saying. Whose name was that they just said?

Whose name did the Father in heaven and Jesus whisper?

Whose name was mentioned in the context of God's grace, His saving plan?

Why...

It was yours.

Grace. Contrary to the devil's assertion, it is impossible to be beyond what encompasses all.

Chapter 4 notes:
[1]Yancey, Philip. <u>What's So Amazing About Grace?</u> Grand Rapids, Michigan: Zondervan Publishing House, 1997, 170-171.
[2]Yancey, p. 70.

Satan's Lies
Your Outlook

Lie #5: "What You Do Doesn't Really Matter"

ANOTHER STORY BEHIND THE STORY

In Luke chapter 10 Jesus gave a special assignment to seventy-two of His followers. After He talked very openly about the challenge and sacrifice of following Him, Luke tells us that Jesus *"appointed seventy-two others and sent them two by two ahead of him to every town and place where he was about to go. He told them, 'The harvest is plentiful, but the workers are few. Ask the Lord of the harvest, therefore, to send out workers into his harvest field. Go! I am sending you out like lambs among wolves'" (vss.1-3).*

So these followers of Jesus went on the road. Two by two they went into villages healing the sick and proclaiming that God's kingdom was near.

When they returned, they were joyful and said to Jesus, *"Lord, even the demons submit to us in your name" (vs.17).* Jesus replied with a glimpse behind the spiritual scenes of life. He gave an answer that lifted up the significance of their two-by-two, on-the-road work in the local villages. He said, *"I saw Satan fall like lightning from heaven" (vs.18).*

This was not a reference to the devil's origin. This was Jesus' eyewitness account of how significant the work of the seventy-two really was. Their healing and proclamation dethroned Satan's dominance in the world. It was a setback for the kingdom of darkness. The work of the seventy-two really mattered! Jesus could see the story behind the story. And it had great significance!

You might think, "Well, they were disciples! They were eyewitness followers of Christ! Of course what THEY did mattered! But what I do is mundane. It's routine. It affects a very small number of people."

And as those thoughts come into your head or come out of your mouth, Satan laughs with glee. If he can get you to believe that what you do doesn't really matter, he has just saved his kingdom of darkness from a crucial setback. He knows that what you do can have eternal consequences. Your life is designed by God to make an eternal impact.

If you think your mundane and routine life doesn't really matter, think again. Let's expose Satan's lie by taking a look at the life of a man named Frank Harwood.

FRANK'S LIFE

Have you ever had baby food or formula stains on your shoulders? Frank Harwood did. No matter how hard he tried to keep his shirts and suitcoats stain-free, all his efforts were vanquished by his nine-month-old baby, Andrea. He would go to the cleaners and that would be her cue to urp something onto his shoulder just when he thought the urping was finished. But that was the life of Frank Harwood.

Andrea was his only daughter. Frank's wife died just two months after Andrea was born. They didn't even know she had cancer. It went very fast, and Frank and Andrea were left to carry on. As you might expect, Andrea became Frank's lifeline. She was his purpose in life. Frank beamed when he talked about her. His co-workers enjoyed seeing the latest pictures of the apple of his eye. They also tried to guess the flavors of his latest shoulder offering. "Looks like mango, Frank," his boss would say as she walked by in the morning. So much for a polished business image.

Every lunch hour Frank hopped in his car and met his mom at the Fair Oaks Nursing Home. It wasn't called a nursing home anymore. It was a "rehabilitation center," but nothing had really changed for his mom during that transition. Frank brought his lunch along and helped feed his mom as they sat together. She had a stroke two years earlier and needed help navigating a lunch tray. Frank was the only person she had. In between bites of his sandwich and spoons full of the soft foods of the day for mom, Frank filled in his mom about Andrea, his job, what kind of day it was, and other world events. Frank also read a devotion to his mom and led in prayer. She was unable to talk since the stroke, but she seemed to enjoy the conversation.

That was the life of Frank Harwood. At the end of the day he picked up Andrea from the babysitter, drove down the main street toward his home, and ended the day with supper, bath time, tucking in, and prayers.

As the years passed there were some changes. Some projects at work were exciting, others not so thrilling. Frank declined two promotions that would have moved him out of the area. He needed to be close to his mom. Frank heard that the neighbor kid who used to play basketball in his driveway went on after a great high school career to play division one college ball and then to the pros. Now he was a high profile person making a lot of money. Frank thought about his own life. He was quite an athlete at one time, but he hadn't played now in years. "I wonder what it would be like," Frank thought.

In time—twelve years to the day after her stroke, Frank's mom died. Frank knew she was with the Lord and at peace, but lunches weren't the same. Andrea had left the baby food messes behind and now was leaving make-up, lip gloss and other girl-types of ornamental items all over the bathroom. She wasn't a baby anymore.

Frank looked in the mirror and wondered about his life. He graduated at the top of his class. Everything he did was successful. Everyone told him that he was going to have a stellar career. He would climb to the top. He would be known. Frank looked in the mirror and saw that the years really didn't bring him public notoriety or reward. They just brought him age! He was working and living in the same place he began fifteen years ago. He was kind of out of shape. He never really was able to get involved in any leadership positions at church or in the community. He was very stable—sometimes it seemed more like a standstill!

But Frank knew that he was doing what he needed to do—and it was good! Learning about barrettes and brushing hair, being a regular at the Fair Oaks Nursing Home, and using his gifts as a faithful employee—not the best dressed, mind you, but faithful—was a good course for his life. It wasn't heroic in the eyes of the world. He wasn't on the cover of "Time" magazine or mentioned in "People's" Fifty Most Beautiful list, but this was the course he needed to go. The truth is, no one else could do it. No one else could be what he was to Andrea and no one else could be what he was to his mom. It was a small corner of the world. The days weren't always exciting. Frank did not leap out of bed each morning with great anticipation. He just kept going, convinced that he was doing His part in God's great plan. Frank was able to see another story behind the story.

ACCEPTING GOD'S ASSIGNMENT

Some people thought Frank was missing out. But Frank knew what he was doing. He had ideas and aspirations. He was intelligent and able. But years ago Frank had decided to accept God's assignment for his life. And he realized along with it, that the assignment may not necessarily be very heroic.

All of God servants have to realize that. Jesus saw what was happening behind the scenes when the seventy-two went out. Frank saw significance in the lives he was reaching. Another person who saw more than meets the eye was Elisha. Elisha and the king of Israel talked in 2 Kings chapter 6. After an amazing lure into the capital city of Israel, the army of Aram was there for the taking. The king asked eagerly, "Shall I kill them? Shall I kill them?"(vs.21) But there was no fire from heaven. There was no earthshaking battle. There was no history making heroics. Elisha spoke for God and told the king, "Feed them supper and send them home."

God may call you to conquer a nation. Or He may call you to make a meal. The question is: Will you accept God's assignment? Will you rejoice in it? Will you throw all your energy, know-how and commitment into it? Will you glorify God and do what He lays before you? Will you trust that what you do really does matter?

SATAN'S LIE

The devil wants to convince you that what you do is worthless, that it makes no significant impact. He'll tell you that fame matters. He'll tell you that being rich matters. He'll tell you that if your life is small and you are relatively unknown you make no difference at all. This lie can throw you into despair, into complacency, or into carelessness.

As I get older I notice that my desire for recognition increases. After all, I've put all my energy into raising my kids.

I've given more than my fair share of blood, sweat and tears at work. I've gained experience and insight as the years have gone by. Isn't it time for the "Father of the Year" award? Aren't my children ready to shower me with statements of gratitude and adoration? Shouldn't the people around me hush in silence as I get ready to share a pearl of wisdom? Shouldn't the church I serve decide to give me a big end of year bonus?

Instead, I continue to help with homework, iron out problems and respond to the needs of my kids—their hope is that I'll keep quiet and not embarrass them. Parishioners are still happy if I can keep the sermon short. Members of my congregation are generous with their thank you's, but there's always the next need, the next meeting, the next job to be done. Sometimes I wonder if I make any difference at all!

The devil tries to convince us that we make a difference only if we can SEE the difference or RECEIVE some recognition. That's wrong. I'll never forget the story of the missionary who, after many years of service, was coming back to the United States. He was traveling on an airplane with a well-known politician and a famous sports star. After the plane landed, the missionary saw great crowds of people waiting. As the passengers emerged, they began to cheer. The politician walked out of the plane and the crowd held up signs that said "Welcome Home." He waved to the people, shook hands, and signed autographs before he was whisked away. The sports star was also greeted with loud cheers and clamoring fans. The missionary, who had been giving his life to serve others, walked from the plane to find a dispersing crowd and a volunteer from a supporting church waiting to drive him to some temporary missionary lodging. As they climbed into the man's pick-up truck, the missionary said wistfully to the driver, "Wow, did you see those crowds? I knew I wouldn't get that kind of welcome."

The driver looked at the missionary and said, "Well sir, that's because you're not home yet."

The driver knew that the difference we make, the story behind the story, will be revealed in heaven when Jesus says, *"Well done, good and faithful servant" (Matthew 25:23).* Life is not measured by awards, recognition, or even the visible impact that we can see.

A very difficult truth to hang on to is that most of God's work happens in small ways, in quiet interactions with unknown people. In an essay titled, "No Little People, No Little Places," Francis Schaeffer said:

> "We must remember throughout our lives that in God's sight, there are no little people and no little places. Only one thing is important: to be consecrated persons in God's place for us, at each moment. Those who think of themselves as little people in little places, if committed to Christ and living under his lordship in the whole of life, may, by God's grace, change the flow of our generation."[1]

Think about Jesus' life. Here was the almighty Son of God! How did He spend His days? With a group of twelve insignificant men. Healing people here and there—most of them are unnamed in the Bible. Raising a widow's son. Reaching out to people with leprosy. Socializing with beggars and prostitutes. As an adult, He never went farther than about 65 miles from His hometown of Nazareth. He told most people to keep quiet about the miracles he performed. Many of the people in His life met Him only once, never to see Him again. Then He died a murderer's death outside the city of Jerusalem.

By the world's standards, Jesus didn't do anything significant. The devil would say that what He did didn't matter at all. Jesus worked in small ways, in quiet interactions with unknown people.

Think about your life. Who has had the greatest impact on you? A movie star? A sports icon? A Fortune 500 executive? A powerful political figure? Probably not. As you think about who impacted you most, you probably would answer, "My mom," or "My Dad," or "My history teacher in high school," or "My best friend." Most likely there are no Oscar winners in that group. Probably very few of those people have the Heisman trophy. But they've made a tremendous difference in your life.

One person who inspired me to pursue physical fitness in life was someone whose name I don't know to this day. I was a freshman in high school, training for a bicycle trip with my church youth group. As we rode on a trail through the Chicago area, I turned the corner and almost collided with a runner. I saw him for just a few seconds. He had dark hair, a mustache, and muscles! He didn't look like Mr. Universe, but he looked like he was in all around good shape. He was an "old guy" — probably around thirty-years-old (I'm laughing as I write that!). As I passed by I thought to myself, "That is what I want to be like. When I get older, I want to be in shape." I didn't even know that guy, but he had a tremendous impact in my life!

Before you plunge into despair or drift into complacency because you feel like your life doesn't make a difference, remember that there is a story behind your story. Satan wants to convince you that you make no difference at all, but God shows you that your assignment is of utmost importance. You just may have to wait until you get home to see the impact God used you to make.

You also want to guard yourself against carelessness. This is one mistake I have seen some experienced followers of Christ slide into. As you get older, you may start to think that you can coast into cruise control when it comes to following Christ. You may begin to think that you don't have to pay close attention to your spiritual health, to the way you speak, or to the way you act as God's servant. I've seen pastors throw sermons together with little or no preparation. They think, "I've been doing this long enough. I can wing it."

I've seen retirees grow in negativity, careless and profane language, and poor habits of study and prayer. They think, "I've been working hard for years. I've given more than my share. Now it's time to relax."

I've seen strong individuals stumble in the area of sexual sin. They figured that they outgrew sexual temptation.

All of those situations show that Satan can convince you that what you do doesn't really matter. He lures you into coasting through life. You get careless, and he pounces!

The Bible lets you know that your WHOLE life is important to God. Psalm 90:12 asks God to lead us in valuing our days that fly by so quickly. The Psalmist, Moses, prays that our days will be used wisely, not squandered: *"Teach us to number our days aright, that we may gain a heart of wisdom."*

Think about other servants of God in the Bible. Enoch was 365 years old when he was used to make others aware of the presence of God. He was taken up into heaven. He didn't die. Noah was about two-thirds of the way through his life when he did the whole ark project. That's getting near retirement age for us. Abraham was seventy-five years old when he began his service to the Lord. Seventy-five! He was 100 years old when he miraculously became a father! Can you imagine how long it took him to get up for those 3:00 a.m. feedings? What about other people in the Bible? The key ministry moments of witness, worship and blessing for Isaac, Jacob and Joseph took place just days before their deaths, each of them over 100 years old. And what about Moses, the one who prayed Psalm 90? He was 80 years old when he started to confront Pharaoh. And when Moses died, Deuteronomy 34:7 says, *"[He] was a hundred and twenty years old...yet his eyes were not weak nor his strength gone."* In fact, in his last days

Moses had responsibility over the entire nation of Israel, was overseeing multiple levels of leadership, and was implementing a ministry transition plan with Joshua as the new leader.

So let me ask you, is your life ever washed up? Is there ever a time when what you do doesn't matter? Aren't you always a precious instrument in the hand of Jesus placed exactly where He needs you to be?

When you resist Satan's lie about the value of what you do, you are living a life that runs totally against the expectations and perceptions of the world. A life that trusts God means that each precious day of your life is a day of training and equipping and service in the work God considers very important. This life of faith means that God isn't wasting any of your time. He is training you for purity, for endurance, for witness, for knowing Him, for self-sacrificial love, for discernment, for compassion, for confidence, and for hearing His voice. No day of yours is squandered by God. In fact, as I mentioned previously, the longer you are around, the bigger and tougher job you might get.

Jesus said in Matthew, Mark and Luke, *"If anyone would come after me, he must deny himself and take up his cross and follow me"(Matt.16:24, Mark 8:34, Luke 9:23).* If this is recorded in the Bible three times, you know it's very important. Jesus' statement confronts you with the questions: Will you follow Him into the life He gives you? Will you follow Him into suffering? Will you follow Him in the midst of success? Will you follow Him in the mundane? Will you follow Him when excitement grabs hold of you? Will you follow Him and be faithful as who you are and where you're at right now? Will you accept God's assignment? That was the life of Frank Harwood, too.

OPEN EYES

If you're willing, how do you make it through that kind of life? Frank found out. He was struck by the irony of life in his later years. Andrea was all grown up now. In fact, she was a regular at the Fair Oaks nursing home because she visited every day to help her dad with lunch. Frank was there. Some heart and circulation problems along with Parkinson's disease precipitated his stay in those familiar surroundings. He didn't like being there, but he sure loved Andrea's visits. He loved the touch of her hand, the sound of her voice, the love in her eyes. Throughout each day he prayed—just talked to God, wondered about life, asked lots of questions, and told Him he was ready to be called home. But if God's assignment was to have him stick around a little longer, Frank said he would go along with it. He was not always cheerful about it, but he would go along with it. He would even accept the baby food that was on his shirt again. "Full circle," he thought. This time the food was from Andrea to him.

Frank remembered words from the Bible that filled his soul—words of Jesus, *"Do not be afraid of what you are about to suffer...Be faithful, even to the point of death, and I will give you the crown of life" (Rev.2:10).* He couldn't hold a Bible anymore or see the print, but He could close his eyes and remember. He recalled those starry and still nights when, after Andrea was asleep, he would sit out on the porch and spend time with Jesus. He would read the Word, ask Jesus to take care of his dear wife, relay a message or two to her about Andrea, and then just listen—read and listen. At Fair Oaks, when Frank's eyes were closed, his eyes were really opened—opened to the faithfulness of God and the presence of Jesus with Him still.

Then came the day when Frank Harwood died. His eyes closed on an ordinary day. But at that very moment, his eyes were opened to see the glory of His Savior! And there in heaven Frank, his mom, his wife, and many others took part in a celebration and welcome that Frank never could have imagined. Frank was home. He asked his mom about those twelve years after her stroke—twelve years with limited movement and the inability to talk. How did she make it? She told him about the hymn verses, the Lord's Prayer, and the Bible verses that flooded her mind in those days. Her eyes sparkled with delight when she remembered the devotions he read. And communion. There was a gasp of awe when it was mentioned. The presence of Jesus. His grace. "That's how I made it," Frank's mom said. "My eyes were opened, and I saw that even when there was so much against me, there was much more for me." And all heaven cheered.

That's what Elisha's servant saw. He was petrified by the forces of destruction around him. But Elisha said, *"Don't be afraid. Those who are with us are more than those who are with them."* And Elisha prayed. He prayed that his servant's eyes could be opened. And the servant saw _"the hills full of horses and chariots of fire all around Elisha" (2 Kings 6:17)._

That was the story behind the story. Jesus saw Satan fall like lightning from heaven when the seventy-two did their work. He saw the story behind the story. Their work was of great significance. When Jesus gives you your assignment in life, He gives it with full knowledge of the story behind the story.

You can accept God's assignment only when your eyes are opened. Do you see that what you do—what you are doing right now—really matters? If you are having trouble seeing it, take a close look at the story—the ultimate story—behind your story. Look closely at, as Jesus said, _"what many prophets and kings wanted to see and hear, but didn't" (Luke 10:24)._ Look at God's Son, the Son who gave His life for you, the Son who walks with you in hardship, the Son who was raised from death to life so that you can walk in new life! Look at Jesus, the Forgiver of your sins and the Redeemer of your life. Look at the best friend and ally you could ever have. Look at the one who gave you life, and is trustworthy with that life.

For your life, for your restlessness, for your wondering, for your desire for something more, and for your fatigue under the load you are carrying, God calls you to accept His assignment, and to follow Him with all you've got! Will you do that? Will you do that even if it means restraint, discipline, waiting, hurting, working, and humility?

If you're nervous about that, if the devil's lies are leading you to be dissatisfied or discouraged, let God open your eyes to see the seventy-two followers who went out to serve. Let God show you Elisha, his assistant, and the king. Let God show you Frank Harwood. Let God give you the certainty of His story behind your story. Jesus watches you live and He sees the heavens being shaken. What you do really matters.

Chapter 5 notes:
[1] Francis Schaeffer. "No Little People, No Little Places." Quoted in <u>Refresh, Renew, Revive.</u> H.B. London, Jr., ed. Colorado Springs: Focus on the Family Publishing, 1996, 203.

Satan's Lies
Your Thoughts

Lie #6: "You Need More Than What You've Got"

"There was a rich man who was dressed in purple and fine linen and lived in luxury every day. At his gate was laid a beggar named Lazarus, covered with sores and longing to eat what fell from the rich man's table. Even the dogs came and licked his sores. "The time came when the beggar died and the angels carried him to Abraham's side. The rich man also died and was buried. In hell, where he was in torment, he looked up and saw Abraham far away, with Lazarus by his side. So he called to him, 'Father Abraham, have pity on me and send Lazarus to dip the tip of his finger in water and cool my tongue, because I am in agony in this fire.' But Abraham replied, 'Son, remember that in your lifetime you received your good things, while Lazarus received bad things, but now he is comforted here and you are in agony. And besides all this, between us and you a great chasm has been fixed, so that those who want to go from here to you cannot, nor can anyone cross over from there to us.' He answered, 'Then I beg you, father, send Lazarus to my father's house, for I have five brothers. Let him warn them, so that they will not also come to this place of torment.' Abraham replied, 'They have Moses and the Prophets; let them listen to them.' 'No, father Abraham,' he said, 'but if someone from the dead goes to them, they will repent.' He said to him, 'If they do not

listen to Moses and the Prophets, they will not be convinced even if someone rises from the dead.'" *(Luke 16:19-31)*

TWO MEN'S LIVES

That was a story Jesus told in Luke chapter 16. He introduced two men in the story. One was a rich man. You have to realize that the rich man wasn't introduced as a villain. He was just living his life. He had blessing upon blessing. Jesus said that he was dressed well and feasted in a splendid way every day. The rich man had everything he needed and more. His house was beautiful. His job was fulfilling and profitable. He had friends and family. He had his health. And God loved him. God loved this rich man.

You also read Jesus' introduction of another man. Verses 20-21 tell of poor Lazarus. There at the doorway of the rich man's home *"was laid a beggar named Lazarus, covered with sores and longing to eat what fell from the rich man's table. Even the dogs came and licked his sores."* Lazarus wasn't introduced as a saint. There is no indication that Lazarus was the "Mother Theresa" of the Middle East. In fact, Lazarus may have messed up in life. He may have liked drinking better than he liked working. That could be how he ended up as an old and washed up beggar. Perhaps his family got so fed up with his behavior, they tossed his immobile and emaciated body at the rich man's doorstep in a desperate hope that Lazarus would get a little something to tide him over in his remaining days on this earth. On the other hand, it may be that Lazarus just had a hard life. Maybe things didn't go his way—his business failed, illness took hold, he was victimized by false friends or merciless robbers. We don't know. But Jesus didn't introduce him as a saint in the story. We do know one thing, however. God loved Lazarus. Even in the midst of suffering and hardship, God loved him.

So, here's a question for you: Of these two men, which one do you think had a more difficult time trusting God?

Do you think it was Lazarus?

That would be a good guess. If you have ever experienced hardship in life, if you have ever waited while God seemed to be silent, if you have ever felt abandoned by God, you may have insight into how Lazarus felt. You may be able to relate to the way he felt about God. Every day when Lazarus was hungry and hurting he could probably hear the loud voice shouting inside himself, "God is not doing anything for you! You need much more from Him! Why trust him at all?" He may have even heard that audibly as passers-by assessed his life.

Lazarus is a good guess.

But perhaps your thought was that the rich man would have a more difficult time trusting God.

That would be a good guess, too. If you have ever experienced blessing in life, if you have ever been in the thick of prosperity, if you have ever been on the road of success being able to do it all, you may have insight into the life of the rich man. You may be able to relate to how he felt about God.

Every day when the rich man scanned the stock reports and moved from one activity to another in a very full and complicated life, he could probably hear the loud voice shouting inside, "God is not doing anything for you! You're working hard. You're making it all happen yourself. Why do you need God at all? He may not even exist. He's going to have to outdo you if you're going to trust Him. " The rich man may have even heard those remarks audibly from his colleagues and many admirers as they assessed his life.

SATAN'S LIE: YOU NEED MORE THAN WHAT YOU'VE GOT

These men had two very different lives. But both of them were susceptible to one of Satan's lies: You need more than what you've got. To put it another way: God isn't doing enough in your life.

As you think about your hopes and dreams, as you go through your hurts and disappointments, that lie could be very easy to believe. God isn't doing enough in your life. You need more from Him. When you're on top of the world, when all is going very well, that lie could be very easy to swallow. God is just a bit player in the script of all your life achievement.

But let's dissect that lie a little more. It accuses God of neglect and passivity. It says that God is not involved in the lives of ones who suffer, and that God is, at best, an observer as you put your own life together. It says that God is out of the picture when it comes to the life you live. It says that if God were REALLY the kind of God He should be, He would step up a little bit, end the scourge of suffering, and take some of the load off the hard workers of the world.

Is Satan leaving something out? Let's take a look at what else was going on in the lives of these two men.

WHAT TWO MEN SHARED

Remember I said that God loved the rich man? How do I know? Well, I know that God loved the rich man so much that, in addition to all his wealth, the rich man was given a special gift from God. It was a "love letter" from God, the Bible! The rich man had the Word of God. Verse 31 calls it "Moses and the Prophets." This was a "love letter" with a promise of life and restoration that would last forever. It was a letter that brought the presence of God—strength, hope and a listening ear. It was a letter that offered great purpose for the rich man's life—he could be a light in a dark world. God loved the rich man so much that He was reaching his soul with His living, relevant, life-transforming, Word.

And what about poor Lazarus? He had that love letter too! We know He did because Lazarus went to heaven. How did Lazarus have God's Word? Maybe he had this love letter of God's Word tucked away in his mind since childhood. Maybe he could hear the great promises of life in heaven being read aloud as he lay outside in the streets. Imagine him listening to the precious words of Isaiah 25 as he lay in his starvation and poverty:

"On this mountain the Lord Almighty will prepare a feast of rich food for all peoples, a banquet of aged wine-- the best of meats and the finest of wines. On this mountain he will destroy the shroud that enfolds all peoples, the sheet that covers all nations; he will swallow up death forever. The Sovereign LORD will wipe away the tears from all faces; he will remove the disgrace of his people from all the earth. The LORD has spoken. In that day they will say, 'Surely this is our God; we trusted in him, and he saved us. This is the LORD, we trusted in him; let us rejoice and be glad in his salvation'"(Isaiah 25:6-9).

This was God's life-touching, hope-giving, Word! And Lazarus had it. God loved the poor man so much that He was reaching his soul with His living, relevant, life-transforming, Word.

THE DEFINING MOMENT

It's no surprise that Lazarus didn't last very long. In verse 22 Jesus tells of the defining moment in the poor man's life. Lazarus died. Jesus gives wonderful insight about what happens when a believer dies. *"The angels carried him to Abraham's side."* No waiting—right away in heaven. Jesus painted a picture of a banquet in heaven—perhaps exactly what Lazarus heard from God's Word. After he died, Lazarus got to recline right next to Abraham. This was a thrill! But Abraham was no stranger. Lazarus got to know him through that precious gift, that love letter, God's Word. Abraham was a person of God's promise. So was Lazarus. Through all the hardship, when the loud voices said, "God is not doing enough for you!", Lazarus listened to God's love letter instead. Satan's lie did not carry the day. And when finality came, God was shown to be faithful. He gave Lazarus exactly what he needed, and exactly what was promised.

In verse 22 Jesus also tells of the defining moment in the rich man's life. He died and was buried. Then comes the bombshell. *"In hell, where he was in torment,"* Jesus said. In hell? What happened? God loved both of these men. Both had His Word of life, His love letter. What happened to the rich man?

BUYING INTO THE LIE

He bought into the lie, didn't he? He needed more than what God gave. What God offered was too small. It was too insignificant for his life. The rich man became bored with blessing.

I was reading an article about a contestant in one of the first television reality shows, "Who wants to marry a multimillionaire?". The contestant was a woman from the northern suburbs of Chicago. When asked why she decided to go on the show she said, "I just liked the excitement, the chance of trying something new and different." And she added, "I am so easily bored."

Do you get bored? Same house, same car, same job, same schedule. Sure, they were new and fresh at one time. But they've been around for a while. Yes, some of those things are great blessings. Some of those things are answers to prayer! Your health, new opportunities, second chances. Some of those things may be miracles—miracles right under your nose! But they happened a while ago. You've been living with them for a few years, a few months, a few weeks, or a few days. They're old news. And you get bored. You get restless. New problems come along. You want some new things to happen. And Satan whispers, "You need more from God. He isn't doing enough in your life."

It's easy to buy into the lie. Our sinful nature gets bored with blessing. You can easily ignore God's work in your life. You can also ignore His personal message to you, the powerful and life-giving love letter that God has put into your life—His Word. As time goes by, you can become convinced that if God would only come through a little more—one more sign, one more message, one more opportunity—then you'll be okay. Then you'll be satisfied. Then you'll have the proof that He is really doing something for you. But do you know what you're really doing? You're saying to God, "Let me call the shots. I know what is best in life. I know what is best for MY life."

That's the tone of the rich man in Luke 16. Did you catch how, even in hell, he had no desire for God's help? God wasn't even in the picture for this rich man. Instead, the rich man had a personal achievement plan! It was polite, but it had no room for God's grace. The rich man said, *"Father Abraham, have pity on me and send Lazarus to dip the tip of his finger in water and cool my tongue."* In the rich man's eyes Lazarus was still just a tool to serve him. Maybe Lazarus was a former

82

servant and the rich man wanted to put him back in his place. As the rich man speaks in Luke 16, he uses words that convey arrogance and that give orders. He's in charge, not God.

When plan "A" didn't work, the rich man said, *"Send Lazarus to my father's house, for I have five brothers. Let him warn them, so that they will not also come to this place of torment."*

What did Abraham say? He told the rich man, "What about God's love letter? What about the Word—not Lazarus the beggar, but Moses himself and the prophets? What about the living and active Word of life from God?"

The rich man replied, "No. No, I have a better idea! If someone were to rise from the dead, then they would repent!"

Do you see how the rich man was buying in to Satan's lie? The Word of God wasn't enough. God's plan wasn't enough. God's will wasn't enough. God's gifts weren't enough. God needed to do more.

So, as Jesus told this story, He had Abraham answer in a sad way. Abraham said, "If they do not listen to Moses and the prophets, neither will they be persuaded, neither will they put their trust in God, even if someone rises from the dead." You've got to believe that Jesus was thinking about His own resurrection and how even that wouldn't be enough for so many.

Do you ever miss out on God's grace or close your eyes to His work in your life? Are you ever nagged by the thought that God isn't doing enough in your life? I had the chance to see the Dead Sea Scrolls exhibit at the Field Museum when it stopped in Chicago. It was truly amazing to look at manuscripts of the Bible so ancient, accurate and well preserved. It was moving to read a copy of Deuteronomy chapter five that was over 1000 years older than any copy we had before, and to see that the love letter from God with news of life and salvation was preserved for us: *"I am the LORD your God, who brought you out of Egypt, out of the land of slavery."* Just think, the rich man in Luke 16 may have had a scroll just like that one in his house!

It was also astounding for me to overhear what some people said as they walked through the exhibit and read the translations of the scrolls. I heard one person declare: "They're making this up."

Another chimed in: "Christ didn't exist."

Do you see what happens? Even when we stand face to face with evidence of God's work, Satan lies, "You need more. God isn't doing enough."

TAKE ANOTHER LOOK

But, as you read, I want to invite you to take another look at what God is doing and can do. If Jesus told the story about the rich man and Lazarus and had the rich man going to heaven, it would be very easy to believe. Of course God could reach this man. Of course God provided for him.

84

But, going back to the question I asked at the beginning of this chapter, what is the likelihood that Lazarus would ever trust in God? Through hardship and pain and misery, dogs licking his sores, hunger wracking his body, how could God ever do enough for him?

And yet, God got through. His Word of life, his outstretched arm of salvation, got through. What does that tell you?

What about the worst of your fears? What about the depths of your grief? What about the darkness of your depression? What about the emptiness of your soul? What about your dashed hopes? What about the crushing pressure of your life? What about your heartbreaking disappointments? Can God get through?

You have the same very special gift that Lazarus and the rich man had. In your suffering and in your blessing you have God's love letter, His living, relevant, and life-transforming Word. That's what Hebrews 4:12 calls it: *"For the word of God is living and active. Sharper than any double-edged sword, it penetrates even to dividing soul and spirit, joints and marrow; it judges the thoughts and attitudes of the heart."* You have the promise from God's love letter, *"My grace is sufficient for you, for my power is made perfect in weakness."(2 Corinthians 12:9).* You have God's Word that He *"will meet all your needs according to his glorious riches in Christ Jesus" (Philippians 4:19).*

You have the Word made flesh, Jesus Christ, who lived among us. You have the Christ, Jesus our Lord, who bled and died so He could rescue you from your sin and helplessness. You have the cross and the resurrection, the agony of Jesus and His triumph for you. You have the promise of eternal life, merciful rescue, peace that surpasses all understanding, and restoration for life that so easily crumbles.

You have the love letter too! No matter what is happening in your life right now, you can know that GOD GETS THROUGH!

THE LOVE LETTER

Do you need God to get through a little more? Ask Him. Say, "God, I need you in times of disagreement, in times of weariness, and through bad circumstances. God, I need you when I am burdened by a hectic schedule. I need you through endless practices and overtime and classes. God I need you during prosperity and blessing. I don't want to miss your Word. I don't want to miss what you give. I don't want to miss all you do in my life. I don't want to miss your love letter."

You may have seen the movie, "The Love Letter," with Tom Selleck and Kate Capshaw. Both of their characters, now nearing mid-life and picking up the pieces of broken marriages, try to get together. Tom Selleck's character has always been in love with the character played by Kate Capshaw. He asks her about the postcard that he sent from New York after they had graduated from high school. Puzzled, she went home, dug it out of a memory box and took a look at it. On the outside there was a typical tourist message. She tossed it in a box when she received it years ago. She then looked closely and found that the post card had a little compartment. In it was a note asking her if she would want to spend the rest of their lives together. She missed the love letter!

It's easy to miss. Blessing or suffering can lead us to toss God's love letter into a drawer. Either way our life goes can cause us to buy into Satan's lie that God should be doing much more for us.

In suffering you may think that God has abandoned you. In blessing you may think that it's not worth waiting for God to lead the way. You may not think you need what He has to give.

But God showed that He gets through. The risen Son of God has a lot for you. You're called to hear His voice and to remember His blessing.

It's not easy. In our fast-paced lives there are many voices around us and in us that cry out, "God isn't doing enough in your life!" In my own experience as a pastor I can go on and on about the pressing needs churches face. It's a challenge trying to keep up with staffing needs, with solid support for volunteers, with timely pastoral care, with good communication systems, with building and facility needs, with effective outreach, and with all the possibilities and wonderful open doors God is offering. Trying to keep up is hard. And the temptation to do what the rich man did—to become a me-first, systems only, raw efficiency, money and outcome centered machine—is high. God can be lost in the church and in your life. That's what Satan wants.

But Jesus calls us back to His love letter. He says, "Let me get through. Don't miss me as life rages. Read and hear what I have to say to you. Come to me in prayer. Let me give you life. Rejoice in my blessing. Trust in my strength."

Counteracting Satan's lie is the Son of God with nail-scarred hands and feet. He says loudly and clearly in His love letter to you and me, "I'll give you exactly what you need. I promise I'll do enough."

Satan's Lies

Your Thoughts

Lie #7: "A Christian Never Feels Afraid"

DO YOU FEEL AFRAID?

You've probably heard it before. You're going through an extremely stressful time of life. Uncertainty is gripping you. The welfare of someone you love hangs in the balance. You're waiting, wondering, and exhausted. Then a well-meaning friend or acquaintance or family member decides to talk with you. Somewhere in the conversation you hear that person say this or a variation of this statement: "You never have to be afraid when you trust in God."

Never have to be afraid? But inside you're falling apart with fear! That must mean you're not much of a believer. You must be a second or third class Christian! Maybe you're not one at all.

Even though the person who said it meant well, Satan delights in that cliché. It's tossed around from believer to unbeliever and from Christian to fellow Christian. Some Christians really believe that if they trust God they will never feel afraid. So, they internalize fear, hide it, feel guilty about it, and suffer the feeling of hypocrisy every day. Believers in Jesus who buy into this lie put on happy faces and pretend that all is well. Inside they feel so alone. Their hearts ache as they yearn to share their fears. But Satan works to keep it all inside. If he has his way, there will be no community. There will be no bearing of each other's burdens. There will be no authenticity in relationships. It will all be a show.

Satan wants to convince everyone of a classic lie: A Christian Never Feels Afraid.

REASON TO FEAR

For all the big and tough guys who are reading this book, I'll be honest with you. I don't get afraid very much anymore. It's pretty rare that I'll be scared. After all, I'm a husband and father, the defender of my family, chief spider killer at home, and head boy intimidator for my teenage daughters. But I'll admit there are times I start to waver.

I went to a craft show with my wife a little while ago. It was just the two of us. We hadn't had an outing like that since our kids were born. My wife's been able to go, but not the two of us together. So there we were. I got in line to purchase the tickets. One line turned into many as the group approached the ticket windows. I saw an opening for one of the shorter lines and decided to try to get to it quickly. Wrong move. I was in a group of serious crafters. Two ladies stepped in front of me. They swiftly took the spots and gave me a look that said, "Move over, rookie." That's when I felt it: FEAR. This was not a leisurely pursuit. No light-hearted hobby crafters here. This was a fight for pole position. I backed away.

Later that day as my wife and I meandered through the crowded craft show aisles, I saw a woman with one of those new two-way radio phones. She was communicating with a partner somewhere else on the craft show floor. These ladies had advanced communication techniques. They had a strategy for their craft purchases. That's when I thought to myself with a tremble inside, "Don't mess with a serious crafter."

When do you feel afraid? If you can think of some times in your life when fear grips you, when worry is too much, or when anxiety keeps you up at night, you're in good company. If we were in a big room and asked everyone who felt fear at one time or another to raise their hands, you'd see a roomful of people who admit to being afraid. And we'd be in very good company. Jesus felt the same way. In Luke chapter twenty-two, as Jesus prayed in Gethsemane, we see that He was feeling some first-class fear. The Son of God was afraid.

Matthew records that Jesus told His disciples that evening, *"My soul is overwhelmed with sorrow to the point of death" (26:38).* That's some big-time fear! Jesus could hardly stand the anxiety He was feeling.

When a friend of mine was getting ready to have some very serious back surgery we got together to talk about how he felt. I could see it in his face. He was petrified. He didn't want to admit it, so I read him the account of Jesus in the garden of

Gethsemane. I told him that Jesus' anxiety didn't mean that Jesus was unfaithful. His fear didn't signal a lack of trust in God. It simply meant that Jesus was going through a very difficult time. It's natural for us to be anxious and afraid when difficulty hits. My friend replied, "Okay, I'll admit it. I'm terrified!"

A teacher of mine used to say, "If you want to know what it's really like to be human, just look at Jesus. He's more man than any of us." So let's take a close look at Jesus in the garden of Gethsemane. Following His lead, I'd like to let you know three reasons that followers of Jesus Christ should be the most fear-filled people on earth.

REASON NUMBER ONE

This is how Luke described Jesus' anxiety-saturated evening in the Garden of Gethsemane: *"Jesus went out as usual to the Mount of Olives, and his disciples followed him. On reaching the place, he said to them, 'Pray that you will not fall into temptation.' He withdrew about a stone's throw beyond them, knelt down and prayed, 'Father, if you are willing, take this cup from me; yet not my will, but yours be done'"* (vss. 39-42).

Jesus was going through agony. Verse 44 comes out and says it very clearly: *"Being in anguish, he prayed more earnestly, and his sweat was like drops of blood falling to the ground."*

Anxiety was gripping Jesus. The worry about indescribable physical pain and an excruciating death was too much to bear. The stress of knowing He would be cast away from His Father was crushing Him. The absolute terror of bearing the sin of the world was beyond description. Blood vessels burst near the surface of His skin and blood mixed with sweat. It dripped to the ground as the Son of God felt as if He couldn't make it another moment. Doctors have described this condition in medical articles that analyze the extreme suffering of Jesus. The bottom line was this: Jesus was totally stressed out! He was afraid. In fact, He was afraid for the same reason you become afraid. He stood face to face with the horror and agony of sin.

That's the first reason why followers of Jesus Christ should be the most fear-filled people on earth. The reality of a sin-broken world strikes fear in the heart.

Parents and children are afraid whenever another report of school violence hits the news. The elderly woman is afraid to walk the streets of her neighborhood. The man facing heart surgery is afraid about whether or not he'll make it through. The unemployed father is afraid that if he doesn't get a job soon, the family may lose their home. The student is afraid that she won't' get her homework in on time. The child is afraid that her best friend may not forgive her.

War around the world strikes fear in our hearts. People in violence-ravaged countries wonder if they will live through another day. Countless numbers of people are walking into doctors' offices on the day you read these words and they are hearing the news that they have cancer. Natural disasters are striking terror in the hearts of victims. Automobile accidents are changing lives forever.

The reality of violence, illness, money struggles, personal stress, broken hearts, disrupted lives; the reality of a sin-broken world, a sin-groaning world—what life is like on our own and apart from God, strikes fear in the heart. It's scary to think about what life would be like if God didn't have His hand in our world! What would happen if God wasn't holding back the havoc-wreaking hounds of hell? What would life be like if the Father in heaven wasn't taking care of us, *"not wanting anyone to perish, but everyone to come to repentance" (2 Peter 3:9)*?

But even with God's merciful reach into our world and into our lives, the sin-brokenness of all we experience is enough to make us feel like Jesus did: anguish, anxiety, stress, and fear.

But like the old song, Satan says, "Don't worry. Be happy." Satan tries to dilute the seriousness of sin. You've heard the statements before: "Everyone is really good at heart. People are generally very good and honest. The bad things that take place are really exceptions." The devil wants to give the impression that there is really nothing very wrong in our world. By doing this he wants to convince you that a Savior is really quite unnecessary.

Satan also tries to convince us that things are getting better and better. There is technology! There are medical advances! People are living longer and longer. There are genetic connections for every malady we might come up with. We can fix everything! A pill here, some surgery there, and *voila!* No problems anymore. If things get too difficult, we can get frozen, and scientists will fix us in a few hundred years. Once again, if the devil covers up the fact that we are all dying, that everything decays, he may succeed in leading us away from realizing our need for a Savior.

When the Titanic was built it was the "unsinkable" ship. It was designed and constructed during a time when industrial advances had people believing that there was no stopping what humans could accomplish. Humanity would keep improving to the point of a nearly utopian existence. But the ship sank. Lives ended. The lie of a utopian world was exposed.

The devil wants to lure you into believing that there is no reason to fear the destructive nature of sin. Karl Marx tried to convince people that faith was for weaklings, people who have needless fears about life. He said that "religion is the opiate of the people." According to him, faith was merely a drug that soothed the simple minds and hearts of people who couldn't face life as it really is. He claimed that life with God was a fantasy that would bring artificial contentment to the simple-minded, while the truly strong people would move ahead to achieve their potential and make society a better place.

Unfortunately, Karl Marx had it all backwards. The opiate of the people is the false belief that we can do better and better, that we have unlimited strength, that on our own we can do all things. That's the fantasy. One bout with some severe stomach flu shows us the truth about us. You may have been the strongest weight lifter, the fastest runner, or the most active mom among all room mothers, but when all you can do is barely make it to the bathroom to throw up every half hour, you don't have a sense that life is a movement of constant progress and improvement. No, there's a different kind of movement going on then. Forget about the next development. At that point you'd settle for some dry toast while watching a few old game shows.

God doesn't fill us with fantasies. He gives the straight-up truth: *"All have sinned and fall short of the glory of God"* (Romans 3:23). *"All have turned away, they have together become worthless; there is no one who does good, not even one. Their throats are open graves; their tongues practice deceit. The poison of vipers is on their lips. Their mouths are full of cursing and bitterness. Their feet are swift to shed blood; ruin and misery mark their ways, and the way of peace they do not know"* (Romans 3:12-17). God is talking about us in those verses—human beings in this world. That's not soothing double-talk. That's the strong truth that exposes Satan's lie. When it comes to sin, to death, and to the absolute corruption and agony of a world in need, there is plenty to fear.

In Gethsemane Jesus came face to face with the serious consequences of sin. In just hours he would be abandoned by His Father because of that. Satan's "don't take life so seriously" double-talk wouldn't fly there. Jesus had good reason to be afraid.   When the reality of a sin-broken world strikes fear in your heart, you do too.

REASON NUMBER TWO

Luke 22:43 says, *"An angel from heaven appeared to him and strengthened him."*

Stronger than the fear of sin and death, Jesus had in Him the fear of God.

Back in the 1500's Martin Luther wrote "The Small Catechism." It was a tool to help families and individuals grow in their faith. One section of "The Small Catechism" is the Ten Commandments. Luther wrote out each commandment and followed it with an explanation—life application for the person learning it. The first commandment is: "You shall have no other Gods." Luther's explanation said, "What does this mean? We should fear, love, and trust in God above all things."[1] Each commandment was quoted and explained.

An interesting thing about all of the explanations Luther wrote to commandments two through ten is that they started the same way: "We should fear and love God so that…" Martin Luther wanted to teach people to fear and love God. Fear AND love.

I was having a talk with a group of third graders who just studied the account of the Passover in Exodus chapter twelve. They were shaken up by the news that God *"struck down all the firstborn in Egypt" (vs.29).*

97

"How could God do something like that?" they asked.

Some adults with them said, "We've heard so much about God's love. Why would God do something like this?"

These students and adults were encountering God's justice and holiness. We talked about how God passes judgment on sin, how He does not tolerate evil, and how He doesn't play games with opposition to His plan and will. We talked about fearing God.

The adults were right. We don't hear much about fearing God these days. I mentioned to the kids that there are two reasons to want to be with Jesus forever. One is that He is our loving Savior who gives us life. What can compare to the awesome life Jesus gives? The other reason, however, has to do with the fear of God. Who would want to oppose God and end up receiving His judgment? Who would want to push God aside and suffer the consequence of hell—eternal separation from Him? Who would want to go head to head with God's might and God's holiness? That is a fearful proposition! It is reason to be afraid!

Another nuance of the fear of God is to have deep respect. Fearing God means you humbly acknowledge His power, His authority, His great might, and you humbly receive His good gifts with gratitude and obedience. Fearing God means you are in relationship with Him. You care that He reaches out to you with His outstretched arm of salvation. You honor Him and thank Him for His goodness and grace. You are thrilled and humbled that God would show His mercy to you, an undeserving sinner. You walk with God in respect and honor.

When an angel was dispatched to help Jesus in His time of need, it showed that Jesus was in a humble relationship with His Father in heaven. Jesus had the fear of God in His life.

That's the second reason why followers of Jesus Christ should be the most fear-filled people on earth: they have the fear of God in their lives. They have a relationship with God that includes deep respect and ongoing gratitude.

I heard Mike Singletary, the famous football player for the Chicago Bears, speak at a Governor's Prayer Breakfast in the Chicago area. Mike Singletary is one of the most feared and fierce football players who ever played the game. His tenacious and powerful moves as a defensive player are renowned in football circles. As he spoke at the podium I knew that this man could still level most people physically and take apart the majority of listeners mentally. There was reason to fear him! Yet he spoke to a group of 1600 people as one who is humble before God, as one who is weak and in need of new life and restoration. Mike Singletary was merciful to us. He chose to be in a relationship with us that conveyed the mercy and grace of God.

That's how God approached us. Instead of destroying us, He destroyed His only Son. Instead of having us live in fear, He allows us to fear and love Him. Instead of getting what we deserve, He gave it all to Jesus. Now we fear and love Him like children fear and love a good and faithful father. John summed it up well when he said, *"How great is the love the Father has lavished on us, that we should be called children of God! And that is what we are!" (1 John 3:1)*

What an amazing thing to stand in the presence of the mighty God and have Him love us! How good it is to tremble in gratitude rather than to tremble in dread.

But Satan would rather have you be very casual about God. The devil wants you to view God as the "old man upstairs" or as an irrelevant oddity in human thought. If you are a believer, the devil won't necessarily try to make you into an atheist. He would rather have you get comfortable in your religion. Attend meetings, do good deeds, go to church, enroll in classes. Build some buildings; lobby for the worship style you want; restructure the church constitution. Of course, those are all good things, but Satan wants you to make those things your focus. He wants those things to define your faith. He doesn't want you to fear God, to be in awe of Him, to walk humbly with Him in a dynamic relationship.

"You have nothing to fear," Satan says. "In fact, why don't you join another committee?"

The devil would rather have you busy and distracted than see angels coming to your aid. He would rather have you preoccupied with "God-stuff" than see the fear of God in your life.

100

REASON NUMBER THREE

As Jesus agonized in the garden, Matthew 26:45-46 says that *"He returned to the disciples and said to them, 'Are you still sleeping and resting? Look, the hour is near, and the Son of Man is betrayed into the hands of sinners. Rise, let us go! Here comes my betrayer!'"*

What happened? Why was Jesus so energized and determined to face the agony that awaited Him? He was gripped with fear and anguish in the garden. What happened to change His demeanor and attitude? First He was saying, "Take this away," now he was saying, "Rise, let us go!" Nothing would stop Him from going to the cross. Why?

Because Jesus was afraid that we would be lost without Him.

The third reason why followers of Jesus Christ should be the most fear-filled people on earth is because they fear that some people may be lost.

Satan says, "C'mon, everyone's going to make it. God wouldn't let anyone go to hell. There's no reason to be afraid!"

All the while he is devouring and destroying God's children.

That's what Jesus highlighted as He explained the parable of the sower in Matthew 13. In verses 18-19 He said, *"Listen then to what the parable of the sower means: When* anyone hears the message about the kingdom and does not understand it, the evil one comes and snatches away what was sown in his heart." Jesus goes on to explain how trouble and persecution, worries and the deceitfulness of wealth, choke out the Word of life and make it unfruitful.

Jesus knew that lives were being lost! Some people were opting out of the kingdom. Others were being pulled away from it. This was a matter of life and death—eternal life and death! So Jesus said, "Rise, let us go!" He came to seek and save the lost (Luke 19:10). He was afraid that some of His Father's dear children would perish.

That's why Jesus said to His disciples, *"Go into all the world and preach the good news to all creation" (Mark 16:15).* He gives all of us the urgent task of making an eternal difference in the lives of all people. He gives you one lifetime—not to accumulate lots of stuff; not to become famous, not to make your mark in the business world, not to get into a good school, not just to do a bunch of things—but in all those things, in all you do, to make His difference wherever you go. The follower of Christ doesn't buy into Satan's lie that there is nothing to fear. A believer in Jesus stands up and follows when he hears Jesus say, "Rise. Let us go!" He follows because he is always afraid that there are precious people who are lost and who need to be found.

FEAR AND NO FEAR

Those are three reasons why followers of Jesus Christ should be the most fear-filled people on earth.

Now, of course, I don't mean that Christians don't trust God. I don't mean that we go ahead and worry without seeking first the kingdom of God. I don't mean that we have no hope. I don't mean that believers in Jesus are to be nervous wrecks, biting their finger nails, and whining about the perils of this age. Satan wants you to live in that kind of unhealthy fear. God wants you to have healthy fear.

As Satan tries to lull you into a snooze through life, a denial of reality, God cries out to you, *"Continue to work out your salvation with fear and trembling" (Philippians 2:12).* "Don't believe Satan's lie!"

And with that healthy fear, you can bow before your Savior and Lord. You can come to Him with fear and repentance for sin. You can come to Him with the fear of God and with humble gratitude for His love and mercy. You can come to Him with the fear and urgency that you are the servant of the Lord to reach the lost.

Chapter 7 Notes
[1]Luther, Martin. Luther's Small Catechism. St. Louis: Concordia Publishing House, 1989, 9.

Satan's Lies
Your Thoughts

Lie #8: "You Have All the Time in the World"

TWO VIEWS OF HISTORY

Did you know there are two views of history in this world? One view is that history is cyclical. This view is prevalent in many world religions. The cyclical view holds that everything keeps coming around again. Just as the seasons keep happening, so life will go—with constant renewal and growth. Leaves fall, but new buds come. Flowers whither, but they sprout again. One life dies, but another is born.

There are many expressions of this view of history. Reincarnation is one variation on this theme of cyclical history. Old Testament Baal worship was another variation. The people who didn't trust in Yahweh believed they could actually gain some control or influence over the gods by contributing to the life force of the world. They would sacrifice children to the gods, thereby gaining some life power for themselves. They would offer themselves to temple prostitutes in order to add to the literal life juices that flowed in the greater scheme of things.

People believed this behavior could make them prosper in the coming life cycle. Business would be better. Social relationships would flourish. Crops would be healthy. Livestock would be prosperous. Family would grow.

Round and round people would go, always banking on another possibility to have things go right.

The second view of history is a linear view. The linear view says there was a beginning and there will be an end. History is going from a definite start to a definite finish. Time is limited.

That's the view of history God presents us with in the Bible. On page one His Word says, "In the beginning." On the last page we hear Jesus say, *"I am coming soon" (Revelation 22:20)*. Time will run out.

Satan would rather have you buy into the cyclical view of history. It's an appealing view. You have all the time in the world. You can contribute positively to your next go round. Even if you don't believe in reincarnation, you can take comfort in the fact that your life might be a positive blip in the cycle of continued blips on the radar screen.

Those are comforting thoughts. But the devil wants you to buy into this lie for a destructive reason. He wants your life to be wasted and destroyed. He wants to convince you that you have all the time in the world so he can bring harm to three areas of your life: your soul, your relationships, and your purpose.

Jesus addresses those three areas in Luke chapter twelve. Let's examine what He says about Satan's lie.

YOUR SOUL

Jesus commented on life threatening situations in Luke twelve. In verses 4-5 He said, *"I tell you, my friends, do not be afraid of those who kill the body and after that can do no more. But I will show you whom you should fear: Fear him who, after the killing of the body, has power to throw you into hell. Yes, I tell you, fear him."*

Those were strong words from Christ. He was talking to His disciples about the Pharisees. It was no secret they wanted to kill Jesus and His helpers. The thoughts of opposition toward Jesus are revealed over and over again in the Gospels. Mark 11:18 tells us, *"The chief priests and the teachers of the law heard this and began looking for a way to kill [Jesus], for they feared him, because the whole crowd was amazed at his teaching."* Luke 19:47 says, *"Every day [Jesus] was teaching at the temple. But the chief priests, the teachers of the law and the leaders among the people were trying to kill him."* John 5:18 comments, *"For this reason the Jews tried all the harder to kill him; not only was he breaking the Sabbath, but he was even calling God his own Father, making himself equal with God."*

But Jesus told His disciples that these life-threatening situations were not their number one worry. He said, *""I tell you, my friends, do not be afraid of those who kill the body and after that can do no more" (Luke 12:4).* Those are some very strong words for us to take in.

Have you ever had a life threatening experience? How did you feel?

When I was in grade school, two robbers entered my grandfather's dry cleaning store in Chicago. One of the men pointed a gun at him and demanded all the money from the cash register. My grandfather was a stubborn Greek. He worked hard for what he earned. He had dealt with many people in his life and it pained him to give in to a couple of thieves. But this was a life threatening situation. He slowly reached for the money in the cash register—all the while considering how he might be able to chase these two hoodlums away with a big knife he kept under the counter. But the thieves panicked. They shot him and ran from the store. My grandfather was hospitalized with a gunshot wound that just missed his heart. He never recovered, however. A few weeks later he died. Our family was crushed. I was shocked. How could someone do this to my grandpa? How could they bring that kind of fear and hurt into his life—into all of our lives?

But Jesus said that kind of experience is not the greatest fear! How could Jesus tell us not to be afraid of that?

I remember a time I nearly drowned. When I was a kid I was swimming in a friend's backyard swimming pool. My feet were in an inner tube as I lay on a floating cushion. I fell off the cushion, but my feet stayed in the inner tube. I found myself floating underwater upside down! I couldn't right myself. I was struggling. I was starting to choke on water. Suddenly my feet popped out of the inner tube and I stood up in the water gasping. No one was around to see what happened. I could have died.

But Jesus said that was not what our number one fear should be! What did He mean?

I've had car accidents that could have been fatal. I've waited for test results—would they come back benign or malignant? But Jesus said not to be afraid of what can kill the body and do no more. How could that be?

Jesus made it clear that something is much worse than physical death: the eternal death of your soul. In Luke 12:5 He said, *"But I will show you whom you should fear: Fear him who, after the killing of the body, has power to throw you into hell. Yes, I tell you, fear him."* Jesus was talking about the Almighty God. His words send us back to the previous chapter in this book when we talked about the fear of God.

Notice how emphatic Jesus was. The word for "show you" can also mean "warn you." Jesus uses the word "fear" three times. He says we should fear the one who, after killing the body, has the authority to throw a person into hell. This was no lighthearted teaching. It was a stern warning that made the welfare of the eternal soul a crystal clear priority. Physical death is nothing compared to being thrown into hell, Jesus said. Getting your soul situation right means everything!

That's a constant theme in Jesus' teaching. Over and over again He countered Satan's lie that we have all the time in the world when it comes to the welfare of our soul, our eternal destiny. Jesus said, *"Be on guard! Be alert! You do not know when that time will come" (Mark 13:33). "What I say to you, I say to everyone: 'Watch!'" (Mark 13:37) "Yes, I am coming soon" (Revelation 22:20).*

In 2 Peter 3, the apostle anticipated the lie the devil would promote. He said people would predict that we have all the time in the world: *"First of all, you must understand that in the last days scoffers will come, scoffing and following their own evil desires. They will say, 'Where is this "coming" he promised? Ever since our fathers died, everything goes on as it has since the beginning of creation.'"* The reality, however, is that our souls need to be on high alert: *"But the day of the Lord will come like a thief. The heavens will disappear with a roar; the elements will be destroyed by fire, and the earth and everything in it will be laid bare. Since everything will be destroyed in this way, what kind of people ought you to be?" (vss.3-4, 10-11)*

What is your soul condition? The devil wants you to put that question on the list of items to look into tomorrow. Jesus says, "Today's the day. Now is the time."

If you've been wondering about the welfare of your own soul, I would encourage you to look at the question very seriously right now. Do you think there is no afterlife, no eternity, no heaven or hell? Are you sure? The stakes are high. Helmut Thielicke in his book <u>How to Believe Again</u> said that if you're unsure about the whole thing, it might be wise to consider the odds and make a good bet. If Jesus is wrong, what do you have to lose? If He is right, you have everything to gain.[1] Of course, walking with Jesus means more than just getting a membership in a church somewhere. In order to place your bet on Him you have to listen to His Word, let Him know you'll give Him a try, trust Him with your life, and desire to have a life that lasts forever. You can talk to Jesus right now and ask that He would give you eternal life. Ask Him to lead you and give you the heart to follow. Then start following. Start reading the Bible. Begin with one of the stories of His life—Matthew, Mark, Luke, or John. Pay close attention to what He says. Give God's Word a chance to work in your life. You'll be amazed at the results. It won't be easy, but your soul will be secure. You will live in eternal blessing. And Satan's effort to have you live in constant procrastination about the most important matter in life will be foiled.

YOUR RELATIONSHIPS

Jesus went on in Luke chapter twelve to talk about relationships. This is another area of life in which Satan says, "You have all the time in the world." Jesus disagreed. He said in verse 15, *"Watch out! Be on your guard against all kinds of greed; a man's life does not consist in the abundance of his possessions."*

Why did Jesus start discussing what a person's life is all about? Why did Jesus bring up the subject of, in the literal translation, where a person draws his life from? It's because of

111

the question He was asked in verse thirteen. This is what happened:

"Someone in the crowd said to him, 'Teacher, tell my brother to divide the inheritance with me.' Jesus replied, 'Man, who appointed me a judge or an arbiter between you?'" (vss.13-14)

Then Jesus told the person in the crowd what life was really all about. It wasn't about possessions. Jesus was pointing the man back to his relationship with his brother. People were more important than possessions. Relationships were more important than riches.

The Greek language that the New Testament was written in has two words for life. One is *bios.* You recognize that from the word "biology." In the New Testament it refers to possessions, the material needed to sustain life. The other word is *zoe* (pronounced zo'-ay). That's where we get the term "zoology." It refers to actual living. It is the word that captures our being, the essence of life.

That is the word Jesus uses in Luke 12:15 when He says, *"A man's life does not consist in the abundance of his possessions."* That's the word He uses in verse 23 when He says, *"Life is more than food, and the body more than clothes."* That's the word Jesus uses when He says, *"The thief comes only to steal and kill and destroy; I have come that they may have life, and have it to the full"* (John 10:10).

That is the word John uses when he said, *"But these are written that you may believe that Jesus is the Christ, the Son of God, and that by believing you may have life in his name" (John 20:31).* *"And this is the testimony: God has given us eternal life, and this life is in his Son" (1 John 5:11).*

Over and over again God's Word directs us to what life is really all about, its essence, what is truly important. In Luke 12 Jesus made it clear that possessions were not the focus. Relationships were. But do you notice that you tend to feel greater urgency to make a certain amount of money, to save a certain sum, to acquire a certain car, to upgrade your computer, or to buy that newer and bigger TV? Time is of the essence, we're told, when it comes to possessions. But what about people? Satan lies to us when he says, "Oh, people. You have all the time in the world with them."

Years ago I met with a young father to talk about priorities in his life. His kids were still small—not even in school yet. The dad had the tendency to work too many hours. We talked about how life would pass by quickly and how his kids needed their father. He would miss out on meaningful life if he came home late in the evenings and worked every weekend. His kids would miss out on a critical component of their lives if he was gone all the time. The dad agreed, but he didn't follow through with his agreement. Even though I touched base with him regularly, I watched him forsake his family. He made money. He acquired toys. But he was a stranger to his kids. Now the time for enjoying their childhood is past. Satan said this dad had all the time in the world. Satan lied.

I remember sitting with a husband and wife who were having some serious marriage struggles. We worked through a lot and came to a point in which each had to make a commitment to give their all for the relationship. The wife agreed to sacrifice much in her life so she could direct her time and energy to build the marriage. Then I asked the husband if he would give up some of his activities and focus his time and energy on the relationship. I asked if he could make this his number one priority. He said he wouldn't do it. He said no. He walked out on his marriage and children so he could pursue other interests in his life. He bought into Satan's lie: "You have all the time in the world when it comes to your relationships."

I also knew a man who raised his kids as a single parent, gave his all to his wife when he got remarried later in life, and lived as one of the most involved and loving grandpas I had ever seen. I was talking with his daughter one day and asked her about a time in life when her dad had a serious bout with cancer. My question was, "How did that struggle with cancer cause your dad's life to change?" The daughter answered, "It didn't. His life didn't have to change. He had healthy relationships and the right priorities."

After I talked to her I thought, "Wow, that is a life truly on target. When crisis comes, you don't have to change. You just keep going."

Jesus gives you that kind of life. When He said, *"Love each other as I have loved you" (John 15:12),* he wasn't speaking in a generic and ethereal way. He was calling us to truly love each other, to give our all in relationships, to live life as it's meant to be lived. As He loved us—with total focus and self-sacrifice—we are called to love each other.   Relationships matter. They give life. Jesus' relationship with us was and is a saving relationship. He gave His life on the cross so we could have life—now and forever. When you truly love your husband or wife, your child or your parents, your friend or your co-worker, you give life. You bring value to that person. You open the doors for growth. You bring meaning that will be passed on to others. You bring the contagious love of Jesus that will bring more lives into the loving arms of our Savior. You make a difference.

In Ephesians chapter five, the calling of Jesus to love each other is applied by Paul to the marriage relationship. If you give your all, Paul said, amazing things will happen. Eugene Peterson translates Paul's words this way in "The Message:"

> *"Christ's love makes the church whole. His words evoke her beauty. Everything he does and says is designed to bring the best out of her, dressing her in dazzling white silk, radiant with holiness. And that is how husbands ought to love their wives" (vss.25-28).*[2]

Possessions get old and out of style. Money gets spent. Riches dwindle in value. But a relationship is designed so each person is better because of it. We're here to bring the best out of each other, to make each other more beautiful as we show the love of Christ.

In Luke chapter twelve Jesus made it very clear that He does not want you to waste your *"zoe,"* your life, on pursuing possessions, status and things. There is precious little time for the relationships He's given you. Maximize those relationships, focus on them, give your all for them, see the wonders that God will work through them.

The devil wants you to isolate yourself and be distracted with everything that doesn't matter. Don't believe him when he tells you that you have all the time in the world to take care of your relationships. He's lying.

YOUR PURPOSE

After His brief dialog with the man who was having inheritance troubles with his brother, Jesus tackled another area of life Satan tries to waste and destroy: your purpose.

What is your purpose in life? Why are you here?

The answer may be different at different times of your life. There are times when your purpose is to be prepared for what's coming. There are times when your purpose is to serve in a small way. There are times when you are to be devoted to your family. There are times when you may be called to impact a great number of people. There are times when you are called to suffer so you can be a living demonstration of God's faithfulness through trial. There are times when you can't quite pinpoint your specific purpose.

Through it all, however, there is one overarching purpose God has given you. It is to be a steward, to be a servant of God Himself.

You may remember the parable of the talents Jesus told in Matthew chapter twenty-five (verses 14-30). A master was going on a long trip, so he put his servants in charge of all he had. He gave money to each servant. Two of the servants invested their money and gave their master a profit when he returned. One of the servants hid his money. He gave it back to the master, but the master was angry that the servant didn't do anything with the gift he was given. Jesus told this story in the context of letting His listeners know they didn't have all the time in the world when it came to using their gifts. The master would be coming soon. So, Jesus emphasized, DO WELL WITH WHAT YOU HAVE. Use your gifts to build God's people. Return to Him what is of value—changed lives. That's your purpose.

In Luke 12 Jesus talked about the farmer who harvested a great crop. What was his first thought? It was "What about me?" The farmer said in verses 18-19, *"This is what I'll do. I will tear down my barns and build bigger ones, and there I will store all my grain and my goods. And I'll say to myself, 'You have plenty of good things laid up for many years. Take life easy; eat, drink and be merry.'"*

The farmer thought about himself. He was totally wound up in his wants, his desires, and his life.

I would love to criticize the selfish farmer, but too often I'm just like him. I notice as the years go by that I want more for myself. When I was in high school I was happy to have a car— any car! It didn't even run all the time, but I was glad to have it. I had to repair rust, plug water leaks, fix upholstery, and rebuild the carburetor, but I didn't care. I had wheels! Now, however, I feel slighted if my car doesn't have a CD player. I feel like I'm driving a second class vehicle if the upholstery isn't leather. I expect the air conditioning to work well, the rear defroster to clear fog away quickly, the intermittent windshield wipers to keep my windshield dropless when it rains. I expect more for myself.

The same is true for my inner life. I notice new struggles. New desires to be known, respected, and given higher positions creep into my being. After being around for a few years and giving my all to what I do, I notice a new temptation to grasp for authority and to receive recognition. It's a new version of the struggle that starts from day one: me, me, me.

Satan reinforces this focus on self when he says, "You have all the time in the world for everyone else. First things first. It's time to think about you."

That lie makes sense to us. After all, logically, how will we be any good unless we're taken care of first? And who will take care of us except us? How will I get what I want, how will I climb the ladder, how will I receive recognition, if I don't take care of me?

But Jesus offers a different perspective. He says, "I give you all things. Will you trust me to take care of you as you walk with me?"

Romans 8:31-32 says, _"If God is for us, who can be against us? He who did not spare his own Son, but gave him up for us all--how will he not also, along with him, graciously give us all things?"_ That's the certain promise that God will take care of me. He will lead me to where He wants me to go. He will give me what He has in mind. What He provides, where He leads, is all I will ever need. And it will be good, for me and for the world.

Notice that God called the rich farmer a fool (Luke 12:20). The issue of purpose was no lighthearted matter for God. We're not here on this earth so we can enjoy some vacation time before heaven. We're here for a purpose. We are here to do well with what we have, to use our gifts to build God's people, and to return to God what is of value—changed lives.

That's what Jesus was getting at as He continued to quote God in verse 20. God said, _"This very night your life will be demanded from you. Then who will get what you have prepared for yourself?"_ The word for "demanded" means "to ask back from," or "to return." The man's soul was given to him as a trust. That very night he would have to return it to God. How was he a steward of that gift? What of value would he return to God?

119

The answers to those questions are implied in the rest of God's statement. Literally He said, "Then who is it that everything has been made ready for?" The answer? You. Yourself. Your own pleasure and illusion of security. God makes it very clear that when you live for yourself, you end up with less than you could ever imagine.

Jesus used the same word for "prepare" or "make ready" when He asked the disciples to prepare the Passover meal in Luke 22:8. Jesus said to Peter and John, *"Go and make preparations for us to eat the Passover."* The word carries a servant-oriented theme. In the parable of the rich farmer, God was asking the rich man about whom he really served in life. The answer again: You. Yourself. Your life was a waste.

That's what Satan wants for your life. Satan says that you're doing the right thing if you live like that. You're looking out for number one. You're doing what no one else would ever do for you. God calls a person who lives like that a fool. God lets you know that you miss your purpose in life if you think you have all the time in the world to give attention to others, and, instead, focus only on yourself. God reveals that strategy as one of Satan's lies.

WALKING THE LINE

Your soul, your relationships, and your purpose: the devil wants to ruin them all. What can you do to prevent it? Remember at the beginning of this chapter I talked about the two views of history. The linear view of the Bible lets you know there is an urgency and importance for your every moment. In that mode of history God calls you to do well with what you have. The key to preventing Satan's successful harm to your soul, your relationships, and your purpose, is to live the way God has given you to live. In Jesus He redeemed you. In Christ He made you a new creation. Now He calls you to live that life well.

When I was younger, my older brother and I were opposites when it came to using gifts we received. One year each of us got a transistor radio for Christmas. We loved the radio. It was just what each of us wanted. My brother treasured his radio. He kept it in its original box. He took it out carefully to listen to it once in a while, but most of the time guarded it from harm. Years later, when the AM radio was out of style and technology passed it by, my brother still had a perfectly preserved transistor radio in its original box. But no one wanted it. It was of no use anymore.

When I got my radio, I listened to it over and over. I wore out the earplug device by listening to ball games secretly in bed at night. The box became tattered. Finally I threw it away. The vinyl case was torn when I kept putting the radio in my backpack so I could bring it to school. Cracks developed in the radio body. Then one day, in response to my growing curiosity about electronic devices, I took the radio apart. I had pieces everywhere! And I couldn't get it back together. The radio was ruined. I ended up throwing it away.

Each of us did only part of what God wants us to do with our gifts. My brother got the treasuring part right, but he never fully used the gift. I got the use part right, but I went too far and abused the gift. God lets you know that time is of the essence to do well with what you have. Treasure your soul, your relationships, and your purpose, but don't stash them away for use at a later date. That date may never come. Use these precious gifts from God for what they are intended. But don't believe you have all the time in the world to abuse them and reclaim them later. That time may not be available.

Jesus summed up His teaching with verse 21: *"This is how it will be with anyone who stores up things for himself but is not rich toward God."*

Jesus made a contrast between "storing up" and "being rich toward." The word for storing up is where we get our word "thesaurus" from. That's a collection of similar words. The word for "being rich toward" paints a picture of extreme generosity and enriching others around you. So Jesus contrasted putting life in a box versus living life by serving generously.

Jesus wanted you out of the box. Time is of the essence.

Notes for Chapter 8

[1] Thielicke, Helmut. How to Believe Again. Philadelphia: Fortress Press, 1972, 12-21.

[2] Peterson, Eugene. The Message. Colorado Springs: Navpress, 1995, 485.

Satan's Lies
Your Thoughts

Lie #9: "I'm in Control"

ARE YOU SURE THE MUD ISN'T IN CONTROL?

Years ago when my wife was 7 ½ months pregnant with our second daughter and our first daughter was not yet two-years-old, we were vacationing and decided to go to a park for a snack and some play time. It was a rainy few days and this park had a covered picnic area. We were going stir crazy staying inside and needed the break. We enjoyed our outing, packed up our things and got ready to go. The rain had started again, but it was nice to get outside. Instead of turning around on the narrow road by the pavilion, we went straight on the road that would loop around to the park exit. We went down a small hill, turned to go toward the exit, started to climb the hill, and realized the car wouldn't go anymore. We couldn't get up the hill. I backed up and took another run at it. Our wheels spun. I got out of the car and surveyed the situation. The road consisted of mud and sand that were soaked by the rain. We had good tires and front wheel drive. It was June. This should not have been a problem! We tried it again and again. No luck. In fact, things were getting worse. The rain was coming down harder and the car was sinking in the mud!

That's how the course of the whole world seems at times, doesn't it? Sinking, sinking, sinking. Sinking in the mud of difficulty and trial. Stuck in the clutches of terrible things: evil, violence, disaster, starvation, illness, tyranny, and death.

It makes you wonder who really is in control.

In Luke 22 Jesus made a comment about Satan's activity to Peter: *"Simon, Simon, Satan has asked to sift you as wheat" (vs. 31).* No surprise, right? Peter would be like the rest of us—stuck in the mud. He would be squeezed in the grip of the devil's evil hand. It's par for the course. Satan rears his ugly head and another servant of God suffers. Sometimes it seems like Satan is in control.

Sifting as wheat refers to how the devil wanted to treat Peter. I saw sifting in action when I was visiting some West African villages. The ladies of the village would stand up and pour the grain from one bowl raised in the air into another bowl placed on the ground. The wind would blow the dried chaff away as the grain fell into the bowl. Over and over the grain would be poured into the air.

That's what Satan wanted to do with Peter. He wanted to toss Peter into the air—up for grabs, at the mercy of the blowing winds of the world. Maybe Peter would be too insubstantial to endure. Maybe he would just drift away.

At first you may respond to that evil strategy of Satan by saying, "It figures! There he goes again! The devil is wreaking havoc in Peter's life just like he wreaks havoc in our lives. Watch the news, read the papers, scan the Bible, and what do you see? The devil in control!"

But look again. Did you notice that Satan gets caught in his lie? Jesus didn't say, "Peter, Satan is going to sift you as wheat." He said, *"Simon, Satan has ASKED to sift you as wheat."* The devil had to ask permission!

You remember Job. In Job chapter one we hear the same thing. Satan had to get permission from God to do anything to Job and his family.

Who really is in control? God is. Even in the midst of all the terrible things that happen, the Bible teaches that God is in control. But the next question is: why do all these terrible things happen?

WHY EVIL AND SUFFERING?

First, back to the mud. There I was, trying to get my car out of the mud, with my very pregnant wife sitting in the back seat next to our toddler daughter. I decided to try everything I could. I pushed the car. I rocked the car. I put sticks and rocks for traction under the tires. I dug. I reasoned. But nothing helped. Really, things just got worse. The car was deeper. I was soaked and dirty. My wife was not feeling very happy. Our daughter was wondering what the hold-up was. And it was about time for lunch. This went on for an hour. At that point in time, I started to consider that, perhaps, I wasn't going to be able to solve this problem.

Peter was helpless, too. Isn't it amazing that while Peter was arguing with all the people he encountered in the courtyard of the high priest (Luke 22:54-62), he didn't even realize he was being sifted! He had no idea he was being tossed up for grabs by Satan. He was not a player in the battle. As I mentioned at the beginning of this book, Peter was the turf. He was the battleground.

But why? Why was this even happening? That's the question that wells up in our hearts when we see suffering and hurt. That's the question we wrestle with when our lives are tossed up into the air, thrown up for grabs by Satan. Why? The Bible gives the answer. Remember what Paul said in Ephesians 6:12, *"For our struggle is not against flesh and blood, but against the rulers, against the authorities, against the powers of this dark world and against the spiritual forces of evil in the heavenly realms."* Remember what Peter said in chapter five of his first letter to believers: *"Your enemy the devil prowls around like a roaring lion looking for someone to devour" (vs. 8).* Remember how the devil's goal is described in Revelation 12: *"Then the dragon was enraged at the woman and went off to make war against the rest of her offspring--those who obey God's commandments and hold to the testimony of Jesus" (vs. 17).* There is a serious battle raging. Along with all the strife and corruption and chaos we bring about because of our sinful nature, the devil and his cohorts are straining to destroy us, to wrest us away from the gracious hands of God.

Well then, how about another question: Why does God LET all these terrible things happen?

126

Let's speculate a little bit. What if Jesus said to Peter, "You know, Satan has asked to sift you as wheat. But I told him to forget it. In fact, I'm tired of his destructive games. My Father told me to annihilate him here and now." Then, WHAM! Satan was gone. Evil was ended.

What would happen? Perhaps a better question is: What wouldn't happen? The cross. The atonement for our sin. The resurrection of Jesus. Victory over death and the grave. Meeting our real need! None of it would happen. We would be stuck in our sinful death spirals, lost from God who loves us so.

Okay, let's revise the plan. Let Peter get sifted. Let Jesus die on the cross and rise again, and THEN put an end to evil and suffering! How about that plan?

What would happen? Well, either God would have to turn us into all-good-doing robots or He would have to end the world. Let's say He continued to respect our free will and simply ended the world after Jesus' resurrection. It would be judgment day. God would look out over all the people and say, "Where are all the believers? Where are the children I love?"

From a small corner a few voices would cry out, "We're over here! We didn't have time to tell anyone else about the Lamb of God who takes away the sin of the world. Sorry, but at least the suffering and evil are gone! At least we're comfortable!"

Okay, that scenario doesn't work either. What if God waited? What if He gave his plan a little bit of time? Back in the

127

early 1900's my grandfather was in the United States Army during World War One. He drove a truck in France. I was always thrilled to hear his stories of seeing bi-planes having dogfights, of close calls as he drove his truck, and of the fun he and his soldier friends would have. This was war, however—a brutal war. One job my grandpa had after the war ended was battlefield cleanup detail. He picked up debris. He also picked up the remains of soldiers. He told the gruesome story of a time he kicked a helmet as it lay on the ground and out rolled the skull of a soldier.

I can imagine during that time, my grandfather saying to God, "This is horrible. Why don't you keep this from ever happening again? Just stop all the evil and suffering right now. It's a good time to do it. The world has just been through a horrible war. Lives are hurting. We could all use your second coming. How 'bout it, God?"

What if God answered yes? It was the twentieth century. Lots of people had already trusted in Christ. God's plan had a lot of time to unfold. The Great Commission was obeyed in many wonderful and life-impacting ways. That would have been a perfect time, wouldn't it?

As you read this you may be thinking, "Yes, that would have been a good time for God to put an end to all evil and suffering. It would have been a great time to come back for judgment. The timing would be wonderful, but..."

But what?

"But I wouldn't have had the chance to know Jesus."

Why did Jesus allow Satan to sift Peter as wheat? Why does God allow suffering and evil to happen at all? The Bible says, *"The Lord is not slow in keeping his promise* (the promise of His return), *as some understand slowness. He is patient with you, not wanting anyone to perish, but everyone to come to repentance" (2 Peter 3:9).*

God has a heart filled with love for every one of us. He doesn't want to lose any of us, so He puts up with sifting and suffering. God even takes evil and suffering into His hands and uses it for ultimate good. We can't always see how He does that, but He knows what He is doing. He has a plan. And, He IS in control.

That's an important fact to grasp. Evil and suffering do not add up to a God who is laying back, helpless, and not in control. Satan would have you believe that, but listen to what Jesus told Peter as he was going to face the sifting of his life: *"I have prayed for you, Simon, that your faith may not fail. And when you have turned back, strengthen your brothers" (Luke 22:32).*

IN CONTROL AND GOING ALL OUT FOR YOU

Without fouling up the eternal plan, Jesus went all out for Peter. **First, He prayed for him**. The reality of Satan's request was that he wanted to sift all of the disciples. The "you" in verse 31 is plural. Jesus knew about Peter's vulnerabilities. So Jesus let Peter know that He prayed for him.

129

The emphasis in verse 32 is on the "I" and the "you." "I prayed for you! The "you" is singular this time. Jesus brought Peter before the throne of grace. The fact that Jesus prayed for Peter was an amazing statement of assurance. Peter saw how effective Jesus' prayers were. Peter knew how serious and focused Jesus' prayer life was. Jesus was on the front lines of the battle for Peter's life.

Sometimes you and I consider prayer as a last resort. "When all else fails, pray," we say. The Bible doesn't portray prayer in that way. Prayer is a first action, ongoing dialog between a child of God and His Heavenly Father. *"Call upon me in the day of trouble; I will deliver you, and you will honor me" (Psalm 50:15).* The prayers of the saints bought a hushed and attentive silence to the heavens (Revelation 8:1-3).

But prayer is not just our action. God lets you know that you, like Peter, have someone on the front lines for you. As you face times of sifting, God lets you know that His Son is also praying for you! Romans 8:34 declares, *"Christ Jesus, who died-- more than that, who was raised to life--is at the right hand of God and is also interceding for us."*

If you ever feel like God has forgotten you, as if He is laying back and not paying attention to your life, think again. Jesus says to YOU today, "I have prayed for you."

Jesus also went all out for Peter by **reminding him of his faith**. He said, *"I have prayed for you, Simon, that your faith may not fail."* Jesus was letting Peter know he had the gift of

130

faith. "Gift" is the key word in that sentence. Jesus wasn't asking the Father to depend on Peter's inner-strength during this time of sifting. Jesus wasn't conjuring up some super sift-fighting stamina that Peter had within. He was letting Peter know that God was holding on to him, that God was doing His doing in Peter's life. That is faith.

Sometimes we think faith is solely our action, our dedication, and our spiritual strength. If you look in the book of Hebrews, however, faith is described in a much different way. Yes, it is ours. God gives us faith. But it is HIS doing in our lives. Hebrews 11:29-30 say, *"By faith the people passed through the Red Sea as on dry land; but when the Egyptians tried to do so, they were drowned. By faith the walls of Jericho fell, after the people had marched around them for seven days."* Who accomplished those great things? Were those wonders rooted in the strength of Moses, or in the know-how of the people of Israel, or in the leadership skills of Joshua? No! God was at work! Faith is His work planted in the hearts and lives of His people. Jesus let Peter know God was at work for Him.

In your trials God reminds you of your faith. In fact, He used Peter to remind you! In 1 Peter 1:6-7 Peter says to believers that *"though now for a little while you may have had to suffer grief in all kinds of trials. These have come so that your faith--of greater worth than gold, which perishes even though refined by fire--may be proved genuine and may result in praise, glory and honor when Jesus Christ is revealed."* You may feel weak and helpless, but God is at work in you. He is faithful. At the right time Jesus will come back and put an end to all sifting, but during the sifting, your Savior is going all out for you.

A third way Jesus went all out for Peter is that **He told Peter the outcome of this trial**. Jesus said, *"When you have turned back..."* Literally, Jesus told Peter, "When you have returned from this sifting..." WHEN, not IF. The outcome was certain. Jesus would win this battle.

What about your time of trial? What about the burden you carry right now, the feeling that your life is up for grabs? What will the outcome be? God lets you know. Romans chapter eight brings great assurance once again:

> *"Who shall separate us from the love of Christ? Shall trouble or hardship or persecution or famine or nakedness or danger or sword? ...No, in all these things we are more than conquerors through him who loved us. For I am convinced that neither death nor life, neither angels nor demons, neither the present nor the future, nor any powers, neither height nor depth, nor anything else in all creation, will be able to separate us from the love of God that is in Christ Jesus our Lord."*

When Peter encouraged believers who were going through suffering, he shared the outcome with them—and with us. He said, *"Though you have not seen him, you love him; and even though you do not see him now, you believe in him and are filled with an inexpressible and glorious joy, for you are receiving* the goal of your faith, the salvation of your souls" (1 Peter 1:8-9). The outcome of the trial is certain. You will not be lost.

The final way Jesus went all out for Peter is that **He told Peter the divine purpose of this sifting**. Jesus said, *"And when you have turned back, strengthen your brothers."* Jesus wanted Peter to know he would use this experience of temptation and failure to strengthen his fellow believers. Transforming power would emanate from this valley of suffering. There were marching orders of witness attached to this trial.

We know that Peter responded. Over and over in his writings he gives witness to the transforming power of Jesus for his lowly life. He says:

> *"But you are a chosen people, a royal priesthood, a holy nation, a people belonging to God, that you may declare the praises of him who called you out of darkness into his wonderful light. Once you were not a people, but now you are the people of God; once you had not received mercy, but now you have received mercy" (1 Peter 2:9-10).*

> *"He himself bore our sins in his body on the tree, so that we might die to sins and live for righteousness; by his wounds you have been healed. For you were like sheep going astray, but now you have returned to the Shepherd and Overseer of your souls" (1 Peter 2:24-25).*

> *"Dear friends, do not be surprised at the painful trial you are suffering, as though something strange were*

133

happening to you. But rejoice that you participate in the sufferings of Christ, so that you may be overjoyed when his glory is revealed" (1 Peter 4:12-13).

"Humble yourselves, therefore, under God's mighty hand, that he may lift you up in due time. Cast all your anxiety on him because he cares for you. Be self-controlled and alert. Your enemy the devil prowls around like a roaring lion looking for someone to devour. Resist him, standing firm in the faith, because you know that your brothers throughout the world are undergoing the same kind of sufferings. And the God of all grace, who called you to his eternal glory in Christ, after you have suffered a little while, will himself restore you and make you strong, firm and steadfast. To him be the power for ever and ever. Amen" (1 Peter 5:6-11).

Peter is speaking from the experience of being sifted by Satan, and from the experience of Jesus going all out for him. With these words God used Peter to strengthen his fellow believers—you and me included! Jesus had a mission for Peter. There was amazing divine purpose to his sifting.

The same is true for you. Satan may toss you up for grabs and claim he is in control. Jesus corrects that assertion by Satan. The ultimate correction was when Satan thought he had Jesus up for grabs. Jesus Himself was sifted like wheat when He suffered and died. But the devil and his angels didn't even have time to start celebrating, for Jesus paid the debt of sin and conquered death. He preached victory to "the spirits in prison"

(1 Peter 3:19). Jesus made it clear that He is in control. As you go through any personal trial, any difficult sifting, Jesus says, "Use this to strengthen your fellow believers. Use this to reach out to ones who do not know Me." Connected to His authority over Satan, Jesus gives you a life with divine purpose. *"All authority in heaven and on earth has been given to me,"* the risen Jesus said to His disciples. *"Therefore go and make disciples of all nations…" (Matthew 28:18-19).* Jesus goes all out for you by giving you divine purpose out of your suffering.

CULTIVATING HONESTY BEFORE GOD

Now remember, we were still stuck in that mud. Throughout this ordeal I had been praying. As one attempt after another failed to free us from the mud, my prayers intensified. In addition to asking for God's help I admitted to Him that I couldn't get that car out. I owned up to the fact that someone else was going to have to get me out of this jam. My answers didn't work. His answers were welcome. I knew God could do a much better job than I ever could. At that point I was willing to run into town a little over a mile away, even though I didn't want to leave my wife and daughter there. I would do whatever God wanted.

Do you see another way God uses sifting and suffering? He uses times of trial to create honest dialog before Him. The devil says, "It's hopeless!" God says, "No, we're just getting ready to talk."

In Luke 22:33-34 the dialog between Peter and Jesus went like this: *"But [Peter] replied, 'Lord, I am ready to go with you to prison and to death.' Jesus answered, 'I tell you, Peter, before the rooster crows today, you will deny three times that you know me.'"* Peter started the conversation with an inaccurate assessment of himself. You and I do that often. We think we're ready to take the next big step. We're ready to serve God in a high-profile way. We're ready to be the leader, the expert, the guru. We want to move beyond the mundane and routine and into the limelight—all for the sake of God's kingdom, of course. But when we assess ourselves that way, we're always mistaken. We're speaking like Peter did. We will never know ourselves as well as God knows us. That's why it's better to let Him move us to where He wants us to be—at His time, in His place. Jesus told Peter that, in reality, he was ready to crumble. Peter was led to honesty before God. After Peter denied Jesus we hear *"he went outside and wept bitterly"* (Luke 22:62). Peter saw that Jesus knew him better than he knew himself. Now Peter was ready to be restored. He was empty and knew he could only live by the grace of God. Peter was poised for the restoration John records in chapter twenty-one of his gospel (vs. 15ff).

God uses trial and suffering to bring you into honest dialog before Him. A friend of mine commented to me once about the blessing of having children. We were both experiencing the gift of newborn children, and we were talking about the nuances of family life. He said, "Kids are a blessing, but not only because they're cute and lovable. Kids expose your weaknesses. If you have a short temper, if you lack patience, if you tire easily, those weaknesses will be brought out and be tested. Kids give you no choice. If you're going to be a good parent, you have to face those weaknesses and grow."

He was right. I never put sleep deprivation in that context before, but he was right. The real blessing of children was that they tested us to the point of having to get our acts together! God works the same way. You may think havoc has gained control, but God uses it to expose the real you, to bring you honestly before Him, and to start growing you. How wonderful it is for God to hear you say in the midst of trial, "Help. I need you, Lord. I'll go your way."

GOD IS IN CONTROL

I was muddy, wet, broken, and willing to do whatever God wanted. But as soon as I got ready to head into town to get help, Cindy and I saw a car driving in the park. It came from a dead-end road down a hill in an area of land that was never used. I ran up the little hill to flag down this 1960's model Chevy. In it were two couples, one in the front and one in the back. Each person was over seventy years old. The lady in the front passenger side rolled down her window. I explained our plight and asked if they could go into town and send a tow truck back. The driver replied, "Why don't we see what we can do." Before I could tell them they didn't have to do anything, the four septuagenarians piled out of the car and into the rain. The women were wearing summer cotton dresses—the kind grandmas wear around the house. The men were in short sleeved shirts. They jogged down the hill toward our car. I couldn't even keep up with them! In my mind I was getting ready to let them know that this is no job for grandmas and grandpas dressed for an afternoon of casual dining. But I couldn't get a word in as they directed my wife to get behind the wheel and as they took up positions surrounding the car. I was barely able to lay a hand on the car when the four of them seemed to lift the car out of the mud and up the hill. After the deed was done they sustained their steady jog, got back in their car and drove off. All I could do was say, "Thank you!" as they left quickly.

My wife and I couldn't believe what just happened. But we were so thankful! We drove into town and stopped at a restaurant for lunch. As we talked about the ordeal, we knew these senior citizens were sent by God. They were either His angels or His very special work crew for us. We never saw them or the car before or since our rescue. One thing we knew: We were stuck in the mud and God came through. In fact, He did a much better job than I would have ever imagined. I never would have prayed, "Dear Lord, send a car of seventy-year-olds to free us from this mire." If I listed one-hundred ways I imagined God might free us, that way wouldn't have appeared on the list! But, as God said, *"As the heavens are higher than the earth, so are my ways higher than your ways and my thoughts than your thoughts" (Isaiah 55:9)*.

God does a much better job than you or I could ever do. Why? Because He IS in control. Satan tries to claim control, but his lie falls apart very quickly. Just look at Peter. Look at the cross. Look at the empty tomb. Look at the spread of the Gospel. Look at the grace of God in your life. Look at the promise of Christ's coming. Satan is lying.

Verse 35 of Luke 22 puts the exclamation point on that when Jesus asked the disciples, *"When I sent you without purse, bag or sandals, did you lack anything?"* The word for "lack" in that sentence is where we get our word "hysteria" from. In a way, Jesus was asking, "When I sent you into this very risky world, was there any reason to panic?" What did the disciples answer? "No. No reason to panic at all. We lacked nothing." That's because the Lord Jesus is in control.

After reading this chapter, when you close this book and step back into this very risky world, will there be a reason to panic? When you encounter sifting, when you get stuck in the mud, when you experience very real and difficult trial, does it mean your life is out of control? You can answer with the disciples, "No. No reason to panic. I will lack nothing. Jesus is in control."

That is an answer of faith as you forge ahead with divine purpose in this difficult world. God promises a great outcome, however. He says, *"In that day they will say, 'Surely this is our God; we trusted in him, and he saved us. This is the LORD, we trusted in him; let us rejoice and be glad in his salvation'"* (Isaiah 25:9). In other words, "God was right! He is in control!"

Satan's Lies

Your Thoughts

Lie #10: "If Jesus Was Your Savior, He'd Do More for You"

MISSING THE POINT AND MISSING JESUS

Jesus reached the high point of suffering and temptation as He hung on the cross. Satan's deception also rose to a crescendo point. This wasn't a wilderness encounter with no one looking. This wasn't a meeting with a vagabond demon in a no-name place in the country. This wasn't a disagreement between friends. At the cross everybody agreed Jesus didn't make sense. Luke 23:35-39 tells us that people stood and watched Jesus as He was crucified. There was a gaper's block of curiosity. Rulers mocked Him. Soldiers made fun of Him. Even criminals assailed Him with insults. Jesus did not make sense to anybody. What was He doing on the cross? Why didn't He do something different?

That's a question you may ask in your life. Why isn't Jesus doing something different—for me?!

The rulers acknowledged Jesus had great power: *"He saved others; let him save himself if he is the Christ of God, the Chosen One" (Luke 23:35).* These rulers saw Jesus perform miracles. They saw the healings. They heard about Lazarus whom Jesus raised from the dead. Jesus saved others! He could do amazing things! Why wasn't He doing more?

The soldiers asked the logical question about this supposed king. Luke tells us: *"The soldiers also came up and mocked him. They offered him wine vinegar and said, 'If you are the king of the Jews, save yourself'"* *(Luke 23:36-37).* What king wouldn't do more? Why would a king, with the power a king had, let himself be killed?

Even one of the criminals made a sensible request: *"Aren't you the Christ? Save yourself and us!"* *(Luke 23:39)* What person receiving the death penalty wouldn't want to escape it? What criminal wouldn't want a stay of execution, a legal loophole to freedom, a group of friends to break in and get him out?

Jesus wasn't making sense to anyone. Why didn't He change His strategy? Why wasn't He doing something more?

The devil tells you that the ultimate deed in life is the deed done for yourself. When you receive benefit, that's the best that can be done. Even if the deed you accomplish is charitable, you should get recognition and, perhaps, a seat on the board of directors. You can be humble, but your financial gain, your gain in prestige, your gain in power, or your gain in recognition should be substantial. That makes the deed worthwhile.

That's why the rulers said, *"Let him save himself!"* That's why the soldiers said, *"Save yourself!"* That's why the thief said, *"Save yourself and us!"* The deed would be worthwhile only if there was personal benefit, only if Jesus was more comfortable (and if WE were more comfortable because of it!).

Think about what you ask Jesus. "Please take my illness away." "Please fix this annoying person in my life!" "Please provide more money for me." "Please give me better hours at work." "Please make my children more obedient." "Please give me a smoother life."

All of it says, "Jesus, do more for ME. If you don't, you really aren't doing enough." And Satan nods his head in agreement. "After all," Satan says, "if He is the Son of God, He should do more for you." But if we believe that lie, we're missing the point of Jesus' being with us. We're not even really seeing Jesus for who He is. Like all those people surrounding the cross in Luke 23, we're losing Jesus in the selfishness of our own plans and ideas.

The same thing happened after Jesus rose from the dead. Remember when Mary Magdalene stood at the empty tomb of Jesus and cried? John chapter 20 tells the story:

> *"Mary stood outside the tomb crying. As she wept, she bent over to look into the tomb and saw two angels in white, seated where Jesus' body had been, one at the head and the other at the foot. They asked her, 'Woman, why are you crying?' 'They have taken my Lord away,' she said, 'and I don't know where they have put*

him.' At this, she turned around and saw Jesus standing there, but she did not realize that it was Jesus. 'Woman,' he said, 'why are you crying? Who is it you are looking for?' Thinking he was the gardener, she said, 'Sir, if you have carried him away, tell me where you have put him, and I will get him'" (vss.11-15).

Mary thought Jesus was the gardener. Why do you think she thought that? I'll give you a hint. In John 19:41-42 you hear this: *"At the place where Jesus was crucified, there was a garden, and in the garden a new tomb, in which no one had ever been laid. Because it was the Jewish day of Preparation and since the tomb was nearby, they laid Jesus there."* Jesus was buried in a garden! And who do you expect to see when you're in a garden? A gardener! Mary assumed that since she was in a garden, the person she would see there would be a gardener.

But you know it wasn't a gardener. It was Jesus. How could she miss Jesus? I assure you, it happens all the time.

When you're at the mall who do you expect to see? Frenzied shoppers! When you're at school who do you expect to see? Crowds of students! When you're in traffic who do you expect to see? Crazy drivers! When you're in a restaurant who do you expect to see? Waiters, waitresses and diners! When you're at home, who do you expect to see? Your family, your neighbors, maybe even a few service people, and some guests.

But do you ever expect to see Jesus? He is alive, after all—risen from the dead! But do you still lose Jesus in your ideas of who He should be and what He should do? Do you lose Him like Mary did, like all the people around the cross did?

Jesus said that it happens. In Matthew 25 He spoke to people who ignored Him and said, *"'For I was hungry and you gave me nothing to eat, I was thirsty and you gave me nothing to drink, I was a stranger and you did not invite me in, I needed clothes and you did not clothe me, I was sick and in prison and you did not look after me.' [They answered], 'Lord, when did we see you hungry or thirsty or a stranger or needing clothes or sick or in prison, and did not help you?' He will reply, 'I tell you the truth, whatever you did not do for one of the least of these, you did not do for me'"* (vss.42-45).

Jesus gets lost before our eyes. We live life, hold to our plans and ideas, and miss Him! Jesus gets lost as Satan says, "If Jesus really was the Savior, He'd do more for you. He can't be around! This is ordinary life." You can get to a point in life where your ideas, plans, and priorities are so dominant that you don't expect to see Jesus anymore. He can be right in front of you—just like He was on the cross and in the garden, but you don't think He's in action. You miss Him.

These days Satan's lie takes us even further down the road of life that is against Christ. We not only miss out on Jesus, we make Him routine, dull and boring. Do you ever find that when the Bible readings happen at church you start to tune out? At home, do you ever find yourself thinking, "Should I read the paper or some of the Bible? I think I'll grab the paper. The Bible just doesn't fire me up." Do you ever find yourself thinking, "Church, Sunday School, Bible class—I'm not in the mood."

Satan is good at convincing us that Jesus is boring, and, in many cases, we're good at reinforcing that lie with the way we worship, pray, treat the Bible, and talk about God. Too often we miss the point, and we miss Jesus.

NOTICING THE SAVIOR

Those are some tough challenges. What is the solution? What did Mary do in John 20? Why, realizing her confusion, she picked up a Christian best-seller to straighten herself out, right? No, that wasn't it. Well then, she probably used the latest prayer technique to become one with Christ, didn't she? No. She must have integrated Christian disciplines into her life so she could tune in to Jesus' voice. Uh-uh. Did she go to church, get the latest scoop from her pastor, and then return to the garden to welcome Jesus? Nope. Those things are very good. They are very helpful tools in the life of a follower of Jesus for strength and growth. God may use them to open your eyes, but the only way you are roused from a frenzied or buried or blinded life is by having Jesus call your name.

In John 20:16 Jesus said, *"Mary!"* In that one word, you see the grace of God with full force. "Mary." In tears and sadness, in fear and sorrow, Jesus called her name. "Mary."

The Bible says the same thing about your life. In Isaiah 43 God speaks and says to you, *"Fear not, for I have redeemed you; I have called you by name; you are mine" (vs.1).*

Martin Luther wrote in his explanation to the third article of the Apostle's Creed, "I believe that I cannot by my own reason or strength believe in Jesus Christ, my Lord, or come to Him; but the Holy Spirit has called me by the Gospel."[1]

This is God's grace, His undeserved love, His passionate reach into your life summarized in one word, "Mary." One writer said, "Never was there a one-word utterance more charged with emotion than this. The life that the Good Shepherd has laid down for the sheep has been laid down for each separate sheep; and His resurrection life is now available for every single believer."[2]

Is there anything greater Jesus could do? He calls your name. He saves you. That's what happened to one of the thieves crucified next to Jesus. In Matthew 27:44 we are told that the thieves crucified with Jesus were both involved in the insults: *"In the same way the robbers who were crucified with him also heaped insults on him."* Both were guilty. Both were missing Jesus. But the Holy Spirit opened the eyes of one of the criminals. Maybe it was because this criminal finally knew that he was powerless. Maybe staring death in the face and feeling the pain of suffocation on a cross woke him up. Maybe the thief remembered some of the things Jesus had done. Maybe he saw Jesus' love in action. But he noticed. Finally he noticed this was the Savior. Luke 23:39-42 tells us what happened:

"One of the criminals who hung there hurled insults at him: 'Aren't you the Christ? Save yourself and us!' But the other criminal rebuked him. 'Don't you fear God,' he said, 'since you are under the same sentence? We are punished justly, for we are getting what our deeds deserve. But this man has done nothing wrong.' Then he said, 'Jesus, remember me when you come into your kingdom.'"

Satan's lie was foiled right there at Golgotha! Three things happened in this man's life to foil the lie. First, this thief stopped thinking of his own ideas of personal benefit. His customized Savior for a smooth and problem-free life was erased. This man admitted his guilt: *"We are punished justly, for we are getting what our deeds deserve."* His own way was no longer the way to go. At one time this man killed people for their money. This man was literally hell-bent on getting what he wanted. Now he cast his own way aside.

Second, this man acknowledged his Savior. He is the only person in Luke's crucifixion account who calls Jesus by name. "Jesus," the man said (vs.42). The name means "Savior." Jesus, the man realized, was the one who could do the most important thing in life for him. He finally noticed his ultimate need and that the stakes of life are eternal. There next to him was the One who could accomplish everything necessary to give him a complete life, a life that was really cared for, a life that was saved. So, the thief on the cross said, "Jesus."

Third, the man asked, *"Remember me when you come into your kingdom" (vs. 42)*. A helpless man cried for help. A

148

dying man hoped for salvation. Instead of money, material things, power, and a life of ease, this man saw what really mattered in life. And he asked the only person who could give him this gift. "Remember me." That was a request for grace. Psalm 25:7 quotes David as he says, *"Remember not the sins of my youth and my rebellious ways; according to your love remember me, for you are good, O LORD."* Virtually every time a person in the Bible calls out the words "Remember me!" it is a call for God's grace. It is a person's plea for God's help. The thief on the cross asked for Jesus to do His greatest act for him.

And Jesus said yes. *"Jesus answered him, 'I tell you the truth, today you will be with me in paradise'" (Luke 23:43).* This was love abounding, life-saving, eternal salvation-giving, grace! GRACE! Right there on the cross, Jesus did it all for the dying thief. *"I tell you the truth,"* Jesus began as he talked to the man. The man's eyes must have opened wide. Anyone listening must have immediately given their rapt attention. Jesus only used that phrase before He spelled out an important kingdom principle. And He did just that: *"Today you will be with me in paradise."* It was certain. It was a gift. It was the ultimate. It was accomplished BECAUSE OF the cross. It is what we really need. It is a gift from God. And the thief on the cross noticed.

What about you? Is God calling you to admit that your blueprints for life, your ideas about what is ideal for you, are not the ways you should be going? Is God calling you to acknowledge that you need a Savior—not a convenience giver or plan accommodator. Is the Holy Spirit silencing Satan's lie and urging you to say, "Jesus"? Is God calling you to ask Jesus

149

to remember you? Is the Holy Spirit prompting you to ask not for possessions, not for comfort, not for success, not for the right marriage partner, not for a baby, not for a promotion, not for a new house, not for any of that! Is He prompting you to ask for God's grace in your life? Today, you can say, "Jesus, remember me." And Jesus will reply, "I tell you the truth, today you will be with me. Today, you will receive all I have to give."

What can be more than that?

SPOTTING JESUS AND ALL HE DOES

What if every day you made the commitment to look for Jesus, to really see Him, to notice all that He is doing in your life? One Easter Sunday after the celebration was finished, I decided to do just that. All the church services were completed. The activity had slowed down. I was very tired, and would have loved to get away. But as I read about what happened to Mary in John chapter 20, I decided to take a closer look at my life. Was Jesus on a break after Easter? Was I left to get recharged on my own so I could crank out more sermons and do more pastoral work? I was going to find out. So on Sunday around lunch time I prayed, "Lord, you promised that you wouldn't just blend in. You're alive and active. So this week I want to see you and hear you. And I don't want it to be my imagination or forcing the issue. You have to be very clear. I will watch and listen for you." And I did. Do you want to know what happened?

On Sunday afternoon I heard how my sister-in-law hid 85 Easter eggs in her living room and dining room so her three small children could have a delightful egg hunt. I also got home from church and heard how my wife made a full Easter breakfast for my daughters that morning since one was sick and they had to miss all the Easter doings at our church. I thought of what Jesus said in Matthew 25:40, _"I tell you the truth, whatever you did for one of the least of these brothers [and sisters] of mine, you did for me."_ On Sunday afternoon, I saw Jesus.

On Monday I was called to pray with a grandma who was dying. Surrounding her bed were her granddaughter and other precious loved ones. The room was packed with love. We prayed, "Take her home, dear Lord Jesus." I looked around and saw the faith and trust in Jesus and I thought of His words, _"For where two or three come together in my name, there am I with them"_ _(Matt.18:20)._ That little grandma, who held onto a cross in her hand to the very end, died one hour later. I thought of Jesus' promise in Revelation 22, _"Behold, I am coming soon!"_ On Monday afternoon, I saw Jesus.

On Tuesday I received an e-mail from missionaries we support in Burkina Faso, West Africa. Chris and Sue and their children were planning a trip back to the U.S. for a time of rest. Before their departure, however, they were reaching out to a group in their village. The e-mail said, "After a time of singing, and a message by Maiga (one of the believers in the village), I gave an invitation to the ladies (about 12) to give their lives to Zezi (Jesus). To the resounding praise of the angels, three of the

151

women said yes and one more wants to, but is waiting permission from her husband. Thus we ask you to rejoice with us as the names of Soumai, Asipto, and Sofi have been added to those who are coming to the great banquet feast the Father is holding one day in His Son's honor." That evening I stood in the hallways of my church doing one-on-one interviews with students who were getting ready to make public confession of their faith in Christ. To nearly 40 students I asked, "Will you be able to say with confidence that Jesus is real, that He gave His life for you, and that you want to follow Him your whole life? Can you answer yes to those questions?" Each student looked me in the eye and said, "Yes!" For believers in West Africa and in my town, I thought of Jesus' words in Matthew 10, *"Whoever acknowledges me before men, I will also acknowledge him before my Father in heaven."* On Tuesday, I saw Jesus.

Then on Wednesday, the last full day before I was going to write down what I observed through the week, I visited a nursing home. I was bringing communion to a dear woman there. Over the past several months this once very active and vibrant woman declined in her physical and mental capabilities. She had an amazing attitude and inspired everyone who lived in and visited the nursing home. Now, however, she suffered in physical weakness and with increasing dementia. We prayed. I gave her communion. But it was hard to keep her attention. I noticed the decline. She became distracted. "Who is that man over there?" she asked after communion. "Do you see him? Who is that?"

I didn't see a man.

She then began talking to another person in the room. That's when a man next to me asked if I was this woman's son. "No," I replied. "I'm her pastor."

"What's your name?" He asked.

"Michael," I said.

"Ahhh, Michael. Well, I'm a believer," he said. "My name is John. We need to follow the Lord. The devil roams around everywhere—even here. I fought in the Second World War. I saw a lot of people who needed Jesus as their guard. I suffered a stroke a little while ago. Now I'm ready to go home—you know, home." He pointed upward.

He continued, "I'm ready to go—not to the undertaker, but to the 'uppertaker.'" He laughed. "A friend at church thought of that one. There are people who will go to the undertaker, but I want no part of that. I'm going to the uppertaker."

Here was a man who knew that Jesus did enough. There was nothing more needed from the Savior of the world.

I bid farewell to the woman I visited. I gave her a bright Easter cross that the Sunday School kids made. She still wondered about that man she saw.

John looked me in the eye and said, "Good bye brother in Christ."

I knew on Wednesday I had seen Jesus again. I didn't realize at the time how vividly.

The next morning as I processed all this and got ready to write my observations for the week, I thought about the woman I visited. I thought about the man she saw after she received communion. I thought about Jesus' words in Matthew 28, *"Surely I am with you always, to the very end of the age."* Who was that man? Ruth—that was her name—never ever saw people. She never had that kind of confusion. She was never that insistent about such an experience.

Shortly after our visit Ruth died. That's when it all came together. I finally realized who Ruth saw. She saw Jesus. She was noticing Him all along. The man who Ruth saw had to be Jesus. Jesus came to call her name. I was certain. He is risen, after all. Why would He do anything less for His dearly loved child?

What are you noticing in your life? Instead of buying into Satan's lie that if Jesus really was the Savior He'd do more for you, what if you decided simply to watch for Him in your life? What wonders would you see right before your eyes?

Notes for Chapter 10

[1] Luther, Martin. Luther's Small Catechism. St. Louis: Concordia Publishing House, 1986, 15.

[2] Tasker, R.V.G. Tyndale New Testament Commentaries, John. Grand Rapids: William B. Eerdmans Publishing Company, 1983, 221.

Satan's Lies
Your Actions

Lie #11: "You Have to Get Caught Up"

WHAT IF JESUS DIDN'T SPEAK UP?

"[The apostles] went out and preached that people should repent. They drove out many demons and anointed many sick people with oil and healed them...The apostles gathered around Jesus and reported to him all they had done and taught. Then, because so many people were coming and going that they did not even have a chance to eat, he said to them, 'Come with me by yourselves to a quiet place and get some rest.' So they went away by themselves in a boat to a solitary place" (Mark 6:12-13, 30-31).

What if, in the middle of that hubbub, Jesus didn't speak up? What if He didn't call His disciples to a time of rest? The activity was wonderful. People were being saved and healed and restored. The disciples were thrilled. They were being used in powerful ways. People were coming to them—droves of people! What would have happened if Jesus kept silent?

- Maybe the disciples would have formed a few departments with management teams in place to spearhead the project areas needed, like preaching, driving out demons and healing.

- Maybe they would have coordinated an anointing oil supply and delivery system, outsourcing the tasks so fully stocked resources could be at their disposal.

- Maybe they would have set up appointment calendars and issued "PDA's" with supporting software so all people could be scheduled and coordinated in various need areas.

- Maybe they would have created an overtime schedule to meet rising demands.

- Perhaps they would have formulated a mission statement with core values and strategies so the job could be done, and done right.

- Perhaps they would have brainstormed a bonus vacation package for their families—two weeks of relaxation on the shores of Lake Galilee—in order to compensate for all the overtime hours. If tasks weren't yet completed, each apostle could be contacted by text message and use wireless internet connections to handle any overflow needs while they were gone.

Is that how it would have gone if Jesus didn't speak up? Is that how it would go if we were running the show that day?

SATAN'S LIE: YOU HAVE TO GET CAUGHT UP

I want to let you know that I do believe in efficiency. Responsibility for tasks is critical. Organization is good. But you and I live in an environment that cries out, "Get the job done!" And in this environment, one of Satan's lies rages: You have to get caught up.

This is a lie that compels people to burn the midnight oil, never to take a break, never to disconnect from their tasks. It's a lie that piles guilt on every homemaker who can never get that storage room or closet cleaned out. It's a lie that makes you nervous about driving your newly washed car in the rain or using a room you just cleaned because then you'll get behind again.

Ultimately it is a lie that hurts you deeply in the life God gives you. I would like to highlight two harmful effects of this lie: First, this is a lie that pulls you away from the rhythm of rest and replenishment God intends for your life. Second, this is a lie that distracts you from the true mission God gives you and the reason for your existence.

You have to get caught up.

MISSING REST

The events taking place in Mark chapter six were very busy and stressful. But Jesus didn't tweak efficiency. He called the disciples to rest. They had already accomplished quite a lot. They had just returned from being sent out to villages so they could bring the Good News of salvation to many people. When the activity level kept going up, Jesus let these followers of His know it was time to get refilled.

That is the way God works. After significant kingdom activity takes place, it is time to rest. Remember what happened when God created the world. Genesis 2 says, *"Thus the heavens and the earth were completed in all their vast array. By the seventh day God had finished the work he had been doing; so on the seventh day he rested from all his work"* *(vss.1-2).*

In Exodus chapter twenty God shared this rhythm of rest with the people He saved and loved so much. God said, *"Remember the Sabbath day by keeping it holy. Six days you shall labor and do all your work, but the seventh day is a Sabbath to the LORD your God. On it you shall not do any work... For in six days the LORD made the heavens and the earth, the sea, and all that is in them, but he rested on the seventh day"* *(vss.8-11).* Isn't it amazing that as God gave the Ten Commandments, the ten key and foundational teachings about life, He included a commandment about rest? Do you realize that out of all the commandments, the greatest amount of dialogue from God is devoted to rest? Not murder, not sexual sin, not coveting. Rest! Obviously, this is a very important message from God. God knew, and He wanted to share with all of us, that even though there's much to do for the kingdom, you need a steady rhythm of rest to do it effectively. You need to get rest along the way.

I remember the frustration of getting out of school and into my career. Nothing was ever done! The finality of completing exams and term papers was gone. There were no semesters that ended. Every day the "to do" list grew. Every day projects, emergencies and needs would surface. There was no end to the week. I couldn't rest when I was finished. A finish would never happen! I discovered that I had to rest along the way. Piles of papers, phone calls and tasks would always be there. If I was going to do anything in a God-pleasing way, I would have to get some rest.

God's plan is that your life would have a regular rhythm of rest and replenishment. Near the end of this chapter you'll have a chance to evaluate the rhythm of your life so you can be very intentional about fighting Satan's lie that sends you running. Your evaluation will include the gifts God gave like worship and prayer. Satan tries to distort God's plan for your life. He says, "There's much to do. You can't stop until it's all done! If you do stop, you're worthless because your value is based on what you do." But God says, "I love you already—with an everlasting love! I value YOU. So get some rest. Let me fill your soul. Stop. I want to make sure you are whole for our journey together."

MISSING PURPOSE

God also wants you to be clear about the nature of, and reason for, your existence. Satan wants you to believe that your goal in life is to get everything done. Peace and happiness are reached when everything is perfect, finished and in order. Then, he asserts, you can enjoy life.

The problem is you never get to that point.

Jesus knew there was plenty yet undone in the disciples' lives. They would have many problems to solve and tasks to accomplish. Immediately after the verses above from Mark 6 the disciples ran into a major project—handling 5000 families for supper. Jesus knew rest couldn't be scheduled AFTER all the major projects were done because He knew the true nature of life. The nature of your life is that you are on a journey filled with people, opportunities, surprises, tasks and challenges.

Jesus also knew rest was important because of the reason for your existence. You are here for the ongoing task of bringing life in Jesus Christ to the world. Those two key points about your life—its nature and purpose—make rest an important priority from God in your life.

TURKEY QUIZ

I had a grade school teacher who used to do an amazing thing. Mr. Spannagle was my social studies teacher in fifth through eighth grades. You know how the school year goes— things get pretty intense once you get into late November. You've plowed through chapters. You've had big tests. You've done a project or two. You've crammed a lot of book knowledge into your brain. But you've also seen the first exciting snowflakes fall. You've finished the fifth draft of your

Christmas list. You're dreaming of the Thanksgiving feast and days off that come with it. There is a struggle going on inside your mind. Attention versus distraction. Work versus play. Business versus pleasure.

And that is when Mr. Spannagle would decide to have a social studies pop quiz. A pop quiz! The week of Thanksgiving!

"Put your books on the floor and take out a pencil," he would say in his most serious tone. "I've got a quiz for you today."

The class would let out a collective groan. Books would slam to the floor. Visions of failure made our heads ache.

"Don't turn the quiz over and start until everyone has it," he would instruct. Then the dreaded moment would come. "You may begin."

I remember turning the mimeographed paper over. I looked and was completely surprised. The title on the top of the paper said, "Turkey Quiz." Question number one was: "What is the main ingredient in pumpkin pie?" As I read each line I discovered that all the questions were goofy. It was a fun quiz! The last question usually asked something like, "What are you going to buy your favorite social studies teacher for Christmas?"

And that was it. We laughed. We smiled. Mr. Spannagle grinned as if he really enjoyed this payback to his rambunctious junior high students. And we were done. What a relief! We were given a break. Our tired minds were granted a reprieve. Our teacher let us rest.

God knows you need that. You need a surprise snow day, a meeting that gets cancelled, a "Turkey Quiz." You need a break in life, a reprieve, a rest.

As you read this chapter you may be looking at new goals and new activities for your life. As you think about what you're going to do next, the devil is whispering in your ear, "If you stop and take a breather, if you don't join everything, if you don't get it all done now, if you don't carry it all on your shoulders, you'll fall behind; you'll be second best; you'll be out of style; you'll never measure up."

But God knows you. Your life is filled with people, opportunities, surprises, tasks and challenges. Your life involves more than just busyness; it exists for the ongoing task of bringing life in Jesus Christ to the world. You're not God; you're God's servant. And God's servants need rest.

NO RESUME NEEDED

I think one thing you and I need to be reminded of over and over again is that God's goal for your life isn't for you to take His job one day. He's not pushing you to be on the Omnipotent Being career track. He hasn't put any want-ads in the newspaper. He hasn't announced retirement plans.

Of course, you may live at times as if He did! Busy, frantic, controlling, worrying. A good example of a fellow servant of God who needed rest, but lived as if God was going to retire any day, is Elijah. In 1 Kings 19 the prophet Elijah was stressing out. Added to his list of worries, he just heard that Queen Jezebel was going to kill him if she could track him down. That sent Elijah over the edge. He dove into frenzied activity. The rhythm of verses three through five in the original Hebrew is absolutely frantic. Look at the rapid fire progression of verbs that takes place: "And Elijah saw, and he stood up, and he went for his life, and he went into Beersheba, and he rested his servant, and he went into the wilderness, and he came, and he sat, and he prayed, and he said, 'Enough, Lord!' And he lay down, and he slept."

Those three verses have twelve verbs! Elijah was in fast motion. Where did it get him? One day into the wilderness and collapsing under a lone shade tree, wishing his life was over.

Are you living like you're trying to put together a resume to take over God's job? Are you trying to do it all, be it all, make it all happen? Does it feel like you've accomplished about as much as Elijah did—one day into the wilderness and ready to give up hope? If it doesn't, it will—under your own power.

Look at that list of verbs again. Notice that "prayed" was verb number ten out of twelve. What do you think would have happened if Elijah tried prayer first? Maybe what happened after he prayed! An angel touched him and said, *"Get up and eat."* God provided the food. The angel said it one more time. What happened? The Bible says, *"Strengthened by that food, [Elijah] traveled forty days and forty nights until he reached Horeb, the mountain of God."* Notice that two small meals from God gave Elijah the strength to journey for forty days! God's strength worked forty times better than Elijah's.

What if conversation with God came before commotion in your life? What if prayer was verb number one instead of verb number ten for you? I'll tell you what would happen. God's strength would do wonders because He takes you far. He gives what you need. He lifts you up. He is the God who lets you rest in His strength for your journey of life.

HURRY LESSONS AND HELP LESSONS

The reality that God lets you rest is completely countercultural, isn't it? Our culture is anti-rest! That is the characteristic of this culture I have not liked teaching our daughters. I haven't enjoyed teaching them to hurry. Too often the pace of life is rush, rush, rush. I realize that schedules and time management must be taught, but it seems as if life is going too fast. When you first learn to tie your shoes, you really need extra time. When you're just starting to eat your lunch at school, they should give you more than 15-20 minutes. If you're an adult reading this book, maybe you have the secret desire for nap time in the middle of the day like you had in kindergarten. That probably doesn't exist anymore in kindergarten. It's probably been replaced with advanced spreadsheet design for preschoolers.

I don't like teaching hurry lessons. To see kids get demoralized and overtired and stressed when they should be reading and daydreaming and taking time to smell the roses is very difficult. It feels like I'm perpetuating something that is very wrong. No margins. Get to it. The schedule is tight. This is how life is.

That's why we need more than hurry lessons. We need what Elijah got: help Lessons. On Mount Horeb, God asked Elijah, *"What are you doing here?"* The question may mean something more like, "What brought you here?" or "How did you make it here?"

Elijah replied with his very eloquent litany of all he had done: *"I have been very zealous for the LORD God Almighty. The Israelites have rejected your covenant, broken down your altars, and put your prophets to death with the sword. I am the only one left, and now they are trying to kill me too" (vs.10).* Elijah was good at hurry lessons.

What did God do? He showed His power in earthquake, wind and fire! Then He asked again, *"What are you doing here, Elijah?"*—How did you make it here? Elijah didn't understand God's message. God was saying to Elijah, "Don't you understand that I got you here? Don't you understand that I kept you safe and I led you and I have preserved your life and provided you with miracles this whole time?" God was giving help Lessons. But Elijah responded with his hurry lessons: *"I have been very zealous for the LORD God Almighty. The Israelites have rejected your covenant, broken down your altars,* and put your prophets to death with the sword. I am the only one left, and now they are trying to kill me too" (vs.14).

So God answered again: "Go back. I will provide kings who will help you. I will provide a partner to give you a break. I will let you in on the fact that there are 7000 people who will keep my plan of salvation going. Elijah, I got you this far. I'm still in control. And I'm giving you help."

It's very important to know that along with the hurry lessons you and I get, God gives help lessons. Life is not just all hurry. It is always filled with God's help. Time with God in worship, in prayer, in reading the Scriptures, in community with fellow believers, are all help lessons. They give balance to your life. They clarify your purpose. They remind you about the nature of life and why you're here. They let you know that the only way you can get to where you're going in life is with God's all-powerful help. Like Elijah, you're where you're at this very moment because of God's grace. And you'll get to where you're going because of God's grace. God lets you rest in His strength and in His gracious sufficiency. That's how you get through a life with people, opportunities, surprises, tasks and challenges. That's how you can be part of the ongoing task of bringing life in Jesus Christ to the world. God lets you rest.

DANCING ON DADDY'S FEET

I think the most poignant part of what God did for Elijah is in verse 16. God tells the mighty prophet Elijah to anoint Elisha as a successor. Literally, God said to Elijah, "Anoint Elisha as a prophet underneath you." Underneath. Elijah needed to hear that. Another person sent by God would be supporting him, carrying his weary self.

When my kids were small there would be times we would dance. One of their favorite ways of dancing was to stand on my feet, hold on to me, and let me move them all around the floor. They would be floating along, dancing on daddy's feet.

That's what God was saying to Elijah: "It's time to dance on daddy's feet. Hold on. I'll carry you through this." God let Him rest.

And He lets you rest. For your weary life, for your worried life, for your hurried life, God sent someone to get underneath you, to pick you up, to carry your weary self. He spoke beautiful words in Matthew 11:28-29: *"Come to me,"* Jesus said, *"Come to me, all you who are weary and burdened, and I will give you rest. Take my yoke upon you and learn from me, for I am gentle and humble in heart, and you will find rest for your souls."* Are you facing worries? Jesus carries you. Are you facing sin's condemnation? Jesus carries you. Are you facing heartbreak? Jesus carries you. He went to the cross for you. God said it in Isaiah 46:4, *"I am he, I am he who will sustain you. I have made you and I will carry you; I will sustain you and I will rescue you."* He did that through the Savior given to us, Jesus Christ. God knows that the nature of your life and the purpose of your life are dependent upon the precious gifts of forgiveness, hope, strength, and eternal life. And that is exactly what God gives you. In Jesus, God lets you rest in His strength, in His gracious sufficiency, and in His life-giving support.

Satan is never going to give you a "Turkey Quiz." He wants you to sweat it out, to live out of balance, to be unrealistic about the nature of your life, and to forget your purpose. He says, "You have to get caught up!"

But God says, "Turn your papers over...Surprise!" God gives you rest in Jesus because He has designed your life to be one that is filled with meaningful living to do! You're not caught up because you have more people, opportunities, surprises, tasks and challenges ahead. You have more in store for you as you experience the blessing of the ongoing task of bringing life in Jesus Christ to the world. You're not caught up because you're not done yet.

IT'S A BATTLE

So Jesus said to His disciples, *"Come with me by yourselves to a quiet place and get some rest"* (Mark 6:31).

He said, **"Come with me."** Rest doesn't simply mean a few extra hours of sleep or a week on a warm beach somewhere. Those are great things! But real rest is soul replenishment. You just read the words of Jesus from Matthew 11. Jesus said, *"I will give you rest."* It is HIS yoke that is easy. He alone removes the burden of life and gives you new life. True soul replenishment is not something you can give yourself. Jesus is the one who gives you a new heart and spirit. He alone

168

restores. It is His grace in your life, not your own doing. True rest happens when you see that, contrary to Satan's lie, your value is not based on what you do, but on the price paid for you—the very life of Jesus given on the cross. In Him you are a new creation. You are forgiven. You are embraced with His love. You live a new life that lasts forever. Only Jesus gives true soul replenishment.

Jesus said, *"Come with me **by yourselves**."* This is a personal call to your redemption. Jesus doesn't have a crowd mentality. He calls YOU. He wants YOU to know yourself—your sin, fallenness, failure, need, sadness and hurt. AND He wants YOU to know HIM. Jesus wants you to know how He restores you, forgives you and puts you back together, why you are alive and on this earth. He wants to give YOU rest. As you think about your life, is there balance between tasks and relationships for you? Are you living the mission and purpose God has given you—being His light wherever He has you right now—or are you just trying to get it all done? Are people in your life falling by the wayside because of the things you have chosen to do?

Jesus said, *"Come with me by yourselves **to a quiet place**."* In this noisy world, Jesus opens the door for quiet and focus. You may not be able to get rid of all noise, but you can turn the TV and radio off. You can put the newspaper down. And you can spend time in prayer. You can hear the Word. You can listen to Jesus and be led by His Spirit. Jesus knew that you need to have time of quietness with Him.

169

Jesus said, *"Come with me by yourselves to a quiet place and get some rest."* Jesus calls you to take some Sabbath time. What is your rhythm of rest and replenishment? When do you get rest on a daily, weekly, monthly and annual basis? Remember, Jesus didn't say, "Get caught up!" He said, "Get some rest." Be filled for the journey. That is what Jesus wants for you today. Are you getting regular, soul-replenishing rest along the way? Let's take a closer look.

FINDING YOUR RHYTHM OF REPLENISHMENT

The phrase "your rhythm of replenishment" was an off-hand comment mentioned by Bill Hybels years ago when I heard him speak at a conference. When he mentioned it, it really struck a chord in me. I never thought about it before. I figured I could just keep going. Sure, I would rest here and there when it happened to come along, but other than that I would keep plugging away in life. I was totally wrong. In fact, I was feeling the effects of plugging away. I felt drained. Hollow. Aimless. So I took a look at my "rhythm of replenishment." In other words, I evaluated the way my life was going, checking to see where there were times I could experience the rest God wanted to give me. As you continue to read this chapter, I would like to lead you in evaluating your rhythm of replenishment.

First look at figure 1, the "Annual Evaluation" section at the end of this chapter. You'll notice there is a line with all the months of the year indicated. Draw an "X" on the line where you take some type of vacation. When I first went through this exercise, the only vacation I had was in the beginning of August.

My schedule was 50 weeks solid of work, then two weeks off. That was a red flag. How does your year look? You may notice that the times you feel drained and discouraged correspond with the big stretches of life with no break. Can you do anything about that? Do you need to reallocate some of your vacation time? Do you need to plan a weekend or two away? I highly recommend that you do your all to take at least one extended break each year. It's not just for sleeping in or playing golf. During this time you should do some life evaluation. Ask yourself: How are you doing as a family member? Are you fulfilling God's calling? What about your job, your level of activities, your health? What life changes is God leading you to make? In other words, how are you living out the mission and purpose God has given you in life?

Now take a look at the "Monthly Evaluation" section. Draw an "X" on the line where you have a real break with people in your life, times when you build into relationships with family members or friends. When do you have a date night, family times, or meaningful conversations with friends? How does your rhythm of replenishment look? Are there any times during the month where you truly rest and live out God's plan for your relationships?

Now look at the "Weekly Evaluation" section. God let us know that His recommended rhythm of replenishment in our relationship with Him is to have at least a once a week time with Him and His people. It's a time when He builds His heart into your heart. Through Word and Sacrament in worship, you are changed from a human "doing" back into a human being.

Draw an "X" in the spot where you are able to hear God remind you about who you are.

Now look at the "Daily Evaluation" section. When do you get small portions of nourishment from God on a daily basis? That means reading God's Word and dialoguing with Him in prayer. Put an "X" in the spots where you're getting that rest from God.

So, what do you think? What changes in your rhythm of replenishment is God leading you to make? Do you see places you need rest? Is anything out of balance?

Finally, take a look at the "Long Term Evaluation" section. You'll notice sections that are divided as decades. God established this long term rhythm of rest when He instituted a "sabbatical year" for His people. After seven years, a portion of land would not be used. It would rest. Slaves would be set free. Debts would be canceled. God was very conscious of a longer-term rhythm of replenishment. I've been a runner for a long time. I've read advice that people who run should redo their goals and expectations every decade. All your fastest running times should be forgotten and renewed when you start a new decade of life. It's a good idea. Life is very different at 21, 41, 61, and 81! Perhaps you shouldn't have the same expectations for how much you weigh when you are 45 as you did at 25. Perhaps you should evaluate your prayer life and your Biblical knowledge so you can be truly growing over the long haul. Shouldn't you know more of what the Bible says when you are 33 compared to when you were 13? Perhaps it's very good to take a serious look at what God is calling you to do in this decade of life. Is it time to sacrifice hobbies and focus on being a parent? Is it time to use the financial resources you've gathered for greater benefit to God's kingdom? You may be able to do that now. Is it time to use your job or your life as a student as a forum for Christian witness? Is it time to bring God's influence to the hospital or nursing home you're in? Is it time to learn and prepare for what God may be bringing down the line? Draw an "X" at your decade of life. What does it mean to be there right now as a follower of Jesus?

That's a different approach to life, isn't it? It's life with rest from God! It's life that breaks Satan's hard-driving lie that your life is merely about getting caught up. As you read these words, you may be weary. You may be overwhelmed. I want to let you know that God has real rest available for you right now. Hebrews 4:9 says, *"There remains, then, a Sabbath-rest for the people of God."* Verse 11 goes on to say, *"Let us, therefore, make every effort to enter that rest."* God wants you to remember that you are His beloved child, here for His precious and life-giving purpose. The question is: will you make every effort to have the rest God gives permeate the rhythm of your life? Will you hear the call of Jesus to His servants, the call that captures real life? *"Come away with me by yourselves to a quiet place and get some rest."*

Figure 1

Annual Evaluation

Jan	Feb	Mar	Apr	May	Jun	Jul	Aug	Sep	Oct	Nov	Dec

Monthly Evaluation

Week 1	Week 2	Week 3	Week 4

Weekly Evaluation

Sun	Mon	Tues	Wed	Thu	Fri	Sat

Daily Evaluation

5am	9am	Noon	3pm	5pm	8pm	10pm	Midnight

Long-term Evaluation

0	10	20	30	40	50	60	70	80	90	100

Satan's Lies
Your Actions

Lie #12: "You Should Really Keep Your Mouth Shut"

MASS COMMUNICATION

I would like to begin this chapter by asking you a few questions:

- Do you have internet access?

- Do you have a television?

- How about a DVD player?

- A satellite dish? Cable TV?

- A cell phone?

- A home computer?

- An iPod?

- A phone answering machine or voice mail?

Did you answer "yes" to most of those questions? If you live in the United States, you probably did. Why? Because we are living in the communication age!

But how about another question:

- Do you believe that these technological tools have brought about a new closeness in your marriage, have enhanced your oneness with your children, have deepened your relationships with friends, and, in general, have increased your personal level of joy?

How would you answer that one?

You see what I'm getting at, don't you? We are living in the age of mass communication, but is it really fostering communication? Does it help make you part of a community? Or is it leading to more isolation than there ever has been?

These days a person can travel a great distance, retrieve messages, make phone calls and leave replies, do their banking, fill up their car with gas, purchase needed items, and curl up to watch a favorite movie, ALL WITHOUT INTERACTING WITH ANOTHER HUMAN BEING. You can live much of life without ever hearing even the sound of your own voice!

SILENCE!

That kind of silence is what the Pharisees wanted when Jesus rode into Jerusalem. We read in Luke 19:39, *"Some of the Pharisees in the crowd said to Jesus, 'Teacher, rebuke your disciples!'"* Noise was happening. It was a noise the Pharisees didn't like. Verses 36-38 tell us, *"As he went along, people spread their cloaks on the road. When he came near the place where the road goes down the Mount of Olives, the whole crowd of disciples began joyfully to praise God in loud voices for all the miracles they had seen: 'Blessed is the king who comes in the name of the Lord!' 'Peace in heaven and glory in the highest!'"* That was noise the Pharisees dreaded. They didn't want the message of new life in Jesus Christ to get out. They wanted silence.

At the root of their objections was another lie of Satan. The devil says, **"You really should keep your mouth shut."** The devil wants silence:

- No communication in families

- No sounds of growing relationships

- No noise of settled conflicts

- No discussion of bearing one another's burdens

- No talk of the Good News of Jesus

Silence. Isolation. That's what Satan wants.

I'm a big advocate of communication. As my children grew up, I emphasized the word: COMMUNICATION! We need COMMUNICATION! I wasn't very popular for constantly asking for effective, face-to-face, talk, but I knew it was a need in our home. Silence, letting feelings go underground, half-hearted apologies, and no accountability to each other wouldn't fly.

Jesus made it very clear that silence wouldn't work in His family either. Jesus spoke boldly to those hushing Pharisees. After they told Him to get control of His followers, Jesus said, *"I say to you"*—remember, that's an authoritative statement that grabbed their attention—*"if they are going to be quiet, the stones will cry out."* The word for "cry out" is where we get our word "crazy" from. Jesus made it clear that the rocks would let loose a crazed cheer if everyone else was silenced. In other words, there was no stopping this noise. Jesus commented on His kingdom in Matthew 16:18. He said, *"The gates of Hades will not have strength against it."* Silencing the message of Jesus Christ doesn't work. The Soviet Union tried it. It didn't work. China and other nations are still trying it. It doesn't work. The message of Jesus Christ who changes lives will not be silenced.

So Satan tries another strategy these days. Instead of silence, the devil tosses loads of noise your way. If he can't silence God's work in your life, perhaps drowning it out will work! Do you notice that effort by Satan in your life? Maybe the noise and information overload is isolating you and overwhelming you so much that the help and hope Jesus gives is being driven out of the picture of your life. Perhaps mass communication in your life is swamping you so much that you don't have the time or the energy to see the life impact Jesus has on you and the world. Perhaps being drowned out by the hubbub of the world will become so dominant that Satan will be

178

able to say, "Give up. You haven't got a chance. You'll never get through. It really is better to keep your mouth shut!"

BEAUTIFUL NOISE

But as Jesus said in Luke 19:40, *"I say to you, if they are going to be quiet, the stones will cry out."* The Bible makes clear that God is not going to let His love for you or His saving work in this world be silenced. Wherever Jesus is, there is noise. Have you ever noticed that? In Luke 19 the people shouted, *"Blessed is the king who comes in the name of the Lord! Peace in heaven and glory in the highest!"* That shout of praise is reminiscent of the noise of the angels in Luke chapter two. During a busy night in Bethlehem, the angels cut loose with a song of praise. They shouted, *"Glory to God in the highest, peace on earth, good will toward men."* The Savior was born! It couldn't be kept quiet. Noise and clamor surrounded Jesus as He preached and healed the sick. Crowds followed Him. In chapter 11 of this book you saw that Jesus even had a hard time breaking away for some rest. Everywhere He went there was the noise of God's grace, the noise of lives being made whole, the noise of God with us. On Good Friday, noise accompanied the death of Jesus. The death of Jesus didn't silence the work of God. It turned up the volume! Matthew tells us about it in chapter 27: *"From the sixth hour until the ninth hour darkness came over all the land. About the ninth hour Jesus cried out in a loud voice, 'Eloi, Eloi, lama sabachthani?'--which means, 'My God, my God, why have you forsaken me?'... And when Jesus had cried out again in a loud voice, he gave up his spirit. At that moment the curtain of the temple was torn in two from top to bottom. The earth shook* and the rocks split. The tombs broke open and the bodies of many holy people who had died were raised to life. They came out of the tombs, and after Jesus' resurrection they went into the holy city and appeared to many people" (vss.45-46, 50-53). This entire Biblical account is filled with noise and commotion! This was no quiet hospital room. This was no hushed funeral home. There was shouting, crying out, the tearing of the temple curtain, the rumbling of the earth, even the dead came back to life and proclaimed a new day. It was as if Jesus was a boulder of life tossed into the small pond of death and waves of renewal gushed onto shore. This was beautiful noise!

And the noise kept happening. When Peter and John were threatened and ordered to stop proclaiming Jesus, we hear them declare in Acts chapter four, *"We cannot help speaking about what we have seen and heard"(vs.20)*. It was more beautiful noise of God's gracious and life saving work.

Perhaps you need some of God's beautiful noise in your life these days. Maybe there are too many fights going on in your home, or too much stress, or lots of hurt. Perhaps overwhelming demands are creating the clamor of chaos in your soul. Satan wants you to suffer with it. He wants you to keep quiet and tough it out. But God has a different plan. He has beautiful noise for your life.

BEAUTIFUL NOISE FOR YOUR LIFE

Countering Satan's lie, Jesus has recovered four key statements for your life. These four statements can be the stones that cry out as Satan tries to hush or drown out the work of God in your life and in your relationships. These are not popular statements. They are not easy words to say. Your life can go charging ahead without ever saying these words. But by pushing away Satan's lie that you really should keep your mouth shut and, instead, speaking up, you will see God do wondrous things. You will experience His leadership in your life. You will lead a life free from the burden of grudges and anger. You will open the door for meaningful relationships. And you will make a difference in the lives of the people God has placed in your life.

The first statement is: **HELP!**

I was riding in my car with someone not too long ago. He and I were looking for an entrance to one of the Chicago area expressways. We took a wrong turn and were foiled for the second time. My friend spotted a gas station. Without blinking an eye, he said, "Stop there! They'll be able to help us." That statement shook me to the very core of my male being. Stop for directions? So soon? Where did this guy come from? I have maps. I grew up around Chicago. Give me a few hours and I'll find the entrance to any expressway you name! But he said, "Let's stop and say, **'Help!'**"

You want to do it all yourself, don't you? You want to get the job done, find your way, and carry the load. You want the credit for figuring it all out, for leading the way. You want to be the expert, the one everyone comes to for advice. You want to be worthy of the high salary or the profuse thanks and praise on volunteer appreciation day. Bottom line: You'd rather be the savior than be saved.

But where will that really take you? Can you really do it all yourself? Aren't you really deceiving yourself? Doesn't this strategy make you hollow inside and bitter on the outside? Isn't this just playing the martyr so you can get attention and affirmation? Doesn't shouldering everything yourself stunt your growth as a human being?

Jesus said, *"Everyone who exalts himself will be humbled, and he who humbles himself will be exalted" (Luke 14:11).* Saying "Help!" opens the door to real power, to real learning, to real meaning in life. It's hard to speak up and ask for help. It means admitting you're not self-sufficient. It means becoming humble and vulnerable. It means you depend on someone else. But Jesus said that by saying "Help!" you will be exalted. There will be a better outcome for your life, one He will lead you to.

Satan says, "Keep your mouth shut! Don't do it!" But Jesus says, "Make some beautiful noise! Say it. Go ahead and say it. Ask, seek, knock. Call upon me in the day of trouble!" You can say, "Help!" Jesus urges you to call for help because He knows your real needs. He knows that without Him you would be lost—lost in sin, lost in life that leads only to death, lost in a skewed perspective of what life is all about. So He gave you a gift, a word to say: "Help!"

Psalm 121 says, *"Where does my help come from? My help comes from the Lord."*

Do you need to say "Help!" today? Do you need to pray, "Okay God, here's what's been troubling me, here's what's been perplexing me in my life, here's what's been enslaving me. I need you to lead me, to help me, to save me, to show me the way."? Go ahead then. Stop and ask for help. Don't let the devil keep you silent anymore. Pray. Talk to your husband or wife. Sit down and have that conversation with your child, with your parent, with your loved one. Make an appointment and go to a counselor. Say the word Jesus gives you. Say the word so help can be on the way.

The second statement Jesus recovers for you is **I'M SORRY. I WAS WRONG.**

You may remember the old TV show "Happy Days." The coolest person in the world was on the show. He was Fonzie played by Henry Winkler. On one episode Fonzie messed up. His friends told him he had to say "I was wrong." But he couldn't do it. The words would not come out of his mouth. All he could say was, "I was wr...I was wr..."

Who wants to admit he is wrong? You and I have pride. We have positions to defend. And even if you're ninety percent right but you hurt your wife's feelings in your rightness, you still have a hard time being the first one to openly and humbly say, "I'm sorry. I was wrong for hurting you."

Satan says, "Keep your mouth shut!" But Jesus says, "Make some beautiful noise! Say it. Go ahead and say it. Confess your sins. Admit your guilt. I give you the gift of saying, 'I'm sorry. I was wrong.'"

Those words work wonders. I am convinced that if pastors and people practiced saying those words sincerely, the burdens weighing people down in the church would significantly decrease. Spiritual health would flourish again. But the words are so hard to say. Why? Because they are completely humbling. They empty you of any pride and any claim to control. They make you powerless and at the mercy of another. People go to great lengths to avoid saying, "I'm sorry. I was wrong."

My wife was hospitalized for a life-threatening condition when she was pregnant with our second daughter. After a week's stay, she was about to be released. Her health had been stabilized and she was doing well with the medication that had been given to her. Before she was cleared to go home, however, a nurse accidentally gave her an overdose of medication. Her final blood tests showed dangerous levels of this drug—it was off the charts. Everyone was puzzled, but my wife explained what happened. A nurse had given her too much of one of her medicines. But no one would listen. No one wanted to admit they were wrong. You know how it is these days: there could be a lawsuit! Malpractice! Million dollar settlements! Everyone kept quiet. Finally I called my wife's doctor and told him what was going on. He checked on her throughout the evening to make sure she would be okay. It was

184

a big scare, but the Lord watched over her and our daughter. Both were healthy. But this ordeal added another week of hospitalization to my wife's already extended stay. She was at her wit's end. The illness, the confusion, the runaround we were getting—they were taking their toll. All my wife wanted was to have someone apologize. I decided to talk to the administrative representative from the hospital. As I sat in her office I could see the fear in her eyes. She thought that a big legal mess was looming. I said to her, "I don't want to sue you. All I am asking is that someone apologizes to my wife." That afternoon the nurse apologized, the floor supervisor apologized, and the hospital administrator I spoke to stopped by to apologize to my wife. When I saw her later that day, I could see that she was peaceful. She told me about the apologies. She was ready to move on.

That's the power of saying "I'm sorry. I was wrong." If said with sincerity and backed up by action (the hospital paid for all the costs incurred because of the overdose, funded all the follow-up tests, and checked in when our daughter was born), the words open the door to healing and wholeness for everyone involved.

1 John 1 says, *"If we confess our sins, [God] is faithful and just and will forgive us our sins and purify us from all unrighteousness" (vs.9).* Saying the words is a starting point in your relationship with God. When is the last time you said to God, "I'm sorry. I was wrong."? When is the last time you articulated your faults, your oversights, your bad attitudes, your impure actions, your SINS to God? When is the last time you

185

assessed your life sincerely and backed up that assessment with action? It may be time to do that right now. In addition to the blessing of forgiveness you receive, God lets you practice honest confession with Him, so you can speak those words well with others. God showers you with His forgiveness, so you can look forward to sharing forgiveness with others. Many worship services will include a time to confess your sins. If you breeze through that time thoughtlessly, you are missing an opportunity to practice the healing words Jesus recovered for you. If you go through the motions, you are missing the opportunity to think about who you need to speak those words to when worship is over. God wants to take the burden of anger, conflict and discord out of your life. These words are words to teach your children, to share with friends, to make a standard part of your life. Make the beautiful noise Jesus gives you. Say, "I'm sorry. I was wrong."

The third statement Jesus recovers for you is **I LOVE YOU.**

A few years ago I was leaving a hospital and saw a lady walking out who looked very sad. I asked her if she was all right. She said, "No." She explained that her father was very ill and that she lived far away. She received a phone call that he had taken a turn for the worse and she flew here as soon as she could. She wanted to see him face to face and say "I love you." It had been a long time. But she didn't make it in time. Her father died before she arrived. The yearning in her expression was powerful. Oh, to be able to say the words, "I love you." But now it was too late. She walked away in sadness.

186

I can't count the number of sons who said to me about their fathers, "I never remember him saying "I love you." That pain impacted their entire lives.

I know a husband who tries to get his wife to tell him she loves him, but she resists. She just won't say it.

Those words are powerful, and the devil knows it. He is already enraged about the fact that God said, *"I have loved you with an everlasting love" (Jeremiah 31:3).* He is incensed that Jesus was so blatant about His love for us. He knows that *"God is love" (1 John 4:16).* So he wants you to stop saying the words.

In the movie "Ghost" with Patrick Swayze and Demi Moore, Patrick Swayze's character would never say "I love you" to Demi Moore's character. He would only say "diddo" when she said it to him. After Swayze's character died, he yearned to say "I love you" to his beloved, and he went to great lengths to accomplish that feat.

But on this side of the grave, the words "I love you" can get lost so easily. When you're swamped in life, love can become the last thing you express in words or actions. When your schedule of activities is crazy, the last thing you feel are "warm fuzzies" of love and affection. These days, families find it difficult to set aside time to eat together. Husbands and wives struggle to carve out space in their calendars to see each other—never mind the open time slots to express their love to each other! At the end of the day people collapse into bed, unable to say a thing. Or, at the end of the day, people stay up surfing the web or vegging out in front of the TV. There are no "I love you's" when people go their separate ways. We live in a day and age in which having time for someone else, listening, taking an interest, and sacrificing self, can easily get crowded out. It's just not as urgent as all the other things.

And Satan cheers. He says, "Keep your mouth shut!"

But God guides us to what is most important. 1 John 4 says, *"This is love: not that we loved God, but that he loved us and sent his Son as an atoning sacrifice for our sins. Dear friends, since God so loved us, we also ought to love one another" (vss.10-11).* God leads you to express your love. If you haven't said it in a while, it may seem like an insurmountable task. It may feel awkward. It may feel unnatural. Should you set the stage? Should you have a fancy dinner? Should you call a family meeting? No. Just say it. Speak up. Look that person in the eye and say, "I love you." Don't say it so you can have it said back to you. Say it to express the fact that you are committed to that person's good. You want the best for him or her. That person is a priority in your life. Building your relationship is important. Say, "I love you." And keep saying it. Let the beautiful noise of God's love saturate your relationships. You'll be amazed at what happens.

The fourth statement Jesus recovers for you is **MAY I TELL YOU?**

Peter said in 1 Peter 3:15, *"Always be prepared to give an answer to everyone who asks you to give the reason for the hope that you have."* This isn't a statement that means you are supposed to give orders as a Christian. This isn't a statement that means you don't listen to others; you just speak. This isn't a statement that means you are supposed to play the part of an authoritative God expert. It simply means that God calls you to articulate what He is doing in your life. You give the reason for the hope you have.

If you are wealthy and successful you can say, "May I tell you why? I live by the grace of God." If you have gone through tremendous hurt you can say, "May I tell you how? It has only been with the help of God." This statement Jesus recovered takes us out of individualism and puts us into community. Instead of appearing self-sufficient, we reveal ourselves as dependent on God. Instead of living the illusion of self-made people, we reveal ourselves as vulnerable human beings who share the same needs, who go through the same brokenness that all humans do. "May I tell you?" brings life to people. It brings hope to the hurting. It creates strong bonds. It brings people into the presence of God.

Of course, Satan wants you to keep quiet. This statement is one of the greatest threats to the devil's goals. Any overt talk about Jesus and the hope He gives sends Satan's forces fleeing. "Keep quiet!" Satan says. "Don't embarrass yourself. Don't pry. Don't impose your beliefs on anybody. Keep your mouth shut!" And many believers do.

When was the last time you sat down with your kids and asked, "Do you want to know why I pray and worship and try to show God's love?" Then you told them about your Savior. You told them the reason for the hope you have. You told them how Jesus has impacted your life. When was the last time you sat down with your husband or wife and talked about spiritual needs, what you believe, and where you're at in your faith journey? When is the last time you said to that friend of yours, "Where are you at in your walk with God? What do you believe?" Then you entered into a dialog that has eternal implications.

Satan says, "Keep your mouth shut!" You may feel very comfortable about being the strong and silent type. You may not want to venture into a faith conversation because you don't have all the answers. You may not want to be vulnerable and transparent about your weaknesses and about the way God has helped you. Remember what Jesus said to the disciples as He prepared them for the noisy days ahead:

> *"There will be great earthquakes, famines and pestilences in various places, and fearful events and great signs from heaven. But before all this, they will lay hands on you and persecute you. They will deliver you to synagogues and prisons, and you will be brought before kings and governors, and all on account of my name. This will result in your being witnesses to them. But make up your mind not to worry beforehand how you will defend yourselves. For I will give you words and wisdom that none of your adversaries will be able to resist or contradict" (Luke 21:11-15).*

Jesus says, "Make some beautiful noise! Say it. Go ahead and say it." You can say, "May I tell you?"

TIME FOR NOISE

Those are four statements Jesus recovers for your life. "Help!"; "I'm sorry. I was wrong."; "I love you."; and "May I tell you?" Your mission is very clear. Make some beautiful noise.

Satan's Lies
Your Actions

Lie #13: "You Shouldn't Bother God with Your Problems"

WOULD YOU BOTHER JESUS IF HE WAS ON VACATION?

There was Jesus, close to the shores of the Mediterranean, ready to take the break He was yearning for. Matthew 15:21 tells us, *"Leaving that place* (the region of Gennesaret), *Jesus withdrew to the region of Tyre and Sidon."* It appears Jesus was trying to get away. Matthew tells us that He "withdrew." He tried that a chapter before and ended up feeding the 5000. Now it was time to go a little further northwest. Perhaps He would find some solitude there.

Tell me, would you call Jesus if He was on vacation? Would you text Him? Maybe you'd send an e-mail. He could take care of that at His leisure. But would you bother Him if He was trying to catch a few moments of relaxation?

Satan would say, "No way!" The devil would try to assume the role of Jesus' personal assistant. The devil would look over his reading glasses with shock, check the world's busy schedule on his clipboard, and say in an exasperated but very proper voice, **"You shouldn't bother God with your problems."** There's just one problem with that. Satan is lying.

Matthew tells us that while Jesus was getting away *"a Canaanite woman from that vicinity came to him, crying out, 'Lord, Son of David, have mercy on me! My daughter is suffering terribly from demon-possession'" (vs.22).* This woman was doing exactly what we talked about last chapter. She was making noise—beautiful noise to Jesus. The word for "crying out" is the same word Jesus used to refer to the stones that would sing His praise in Luke 19. As I mentioned, it's where we get our word "crazy" from. This woman was really making a fuss. She used the first statement Jesus loves to hear, *"Help me!" (vs.25)* As you read this account it might seem that Jesus was annoyed. He was slow to respond to the woman. But notice how Jesus stuck with her the entire way.

The disciples were quick to get irritated. Jesus didn't answer yet, but the disciples made haste to give Jesus vacation advice: *"Send her away, for she keeps crying out after us" (vs.23).* The disciples were treating this situation like a car chase from the paparazzi. In the literal translation it sounds like they were saying, "Lose her because she keeps tailing us!"

Satan was rooting for this solution to the "problem." Here was a woman, a Canaanite, and a pest! Back in Bible days those three factors added up to an unwanted encounter— especially for a Jewish person. But Satan's enthusiasm to have this meeting terminated was rooted in another motive. He didn't want Jesus to solve this problem. In fact, He doesn't want Jesus to solve any problem—yours included! Why was this woman so distressed? Her daughter was severely demon-possessed. Satan didn't want the problem solved because HE

194

WAS THE PROBLEM! That's the way it goes in your life too. Satan says, "Don't bother God with your problems"—all the while he is CAUSING problems for you. The devil wants no interference when it comes to the trouble he causes. That's why he tries to dissuade you from approaching God. If God steps in, Satan is history! So the devil sneaks and lies. He tries to make you feel unworthy of God's listening ear. He tries to convince you that your problems are too small. He tries to get you to believe that God is too busy. All the while he is creating havoc and pain in your life—and laughing at your helplessness, delighting in your downcast spirit, and rejoicing in your disappointment with God.

But even on vacation, Jesus communicated His amazing care for all of us. Listen to what happened next. To His disciples Jesus said, *"I was sent only to the lost sheep of Israel."* Then: *"The woman came and knelt before him. 'Lord, help me!' she said. He replied, 'It is not right to take the children's bread and toss it to their dogs'" (vss.24-26).* What happened here? Let me highlight three key points.

THERE IS A PLAN

Jesus didn't answer the woman right away. He spoke to His disciples after they begged Him to get rid of the woman. He told them He was sent for the perishing and lost sheep of the house of Israel. In other words, Jesus was reinforcing God's plan. He was teaching the disciples that God had a great strategy He was unfolding. These words of Jesus drove home two points. First, they gave the disciples the comfort of

195

knowing that Jesus' presence and work were very intentional. They were a fulfillment of God's promises to His people. Even in the craziness of this encounter, even in the middle of this interrupted vacation, the plan of God was still intact. God's kingdom was still advancing according to His purpose and will.

Who doesn't need to hear that teaching? How often do you find yourself in the middle of craziness, situations that are out of control, a life that seems to make no sense? One minute you seem to have total clarity about God's direction in your life. The next moment you're totally puzzled. You need to hear Jesus' words, don't you? There is a plan. God is in charge. When terrible things happen and doubt fills your soul, you need to hear those words, don't you? They may be difficult to hear, but God says, "Trust me. I have a plan." These are words of comfort from our Savior who lets us know our lives are in His gracious hands.

The second point these words of Jesus drove home to the disciples has to do with the nature of God's plan. These words to the disciples would serve as a prelude for what they would soon witness. If they had any thoughts about elitism, about personal power, about individual kingdoms, or about hoarding the glory of Jesus, these words—combined with Jesus' response of healing in verse 28—would bring clarity to the nature of God's plan and will. Remember, God wanted Israel to be a light for the nations. Micah 6:6-8 sums up God's will for Israel:

"With what shall I come before the LORD and bow down before the exalted God? Shall I come before him with burnt offerings, with calves a year old? Will the LORD be pleased with thousands of rams, with ten thousand rivers of oil? Shall I offer my firstborn for my transgression, the fruit of my body for the sin of my soul? He has showed you, O man, what is good. And what does the LORD require of you? To act justly and to love mercy and to walk humbly with your God."

Jesus' priority-one outreach to the people of Israel was meant to create a compassionate, Spirit-filled people who reached out with the redemptive love of Christ. Jesus would live out that plan in front of His disciples here in Matthew chapter fifteen.

GOD LOVES YOU

The second point this encounter makes clear is that God loves you. You may be very familiar with that phrase. "Sure, God loves me," you may answer, "I've heard it a thousand times before." My question for you is: Do you really know what that means? Jesus entered into dialog with this Canaanite woman. He stuck with her. He didn't send her away. *"The woman came and knelt before him. 'Lord, help me!' she said. He replied, 'It is not right to take the children's bread and toss it to their dogs.'"* Jesus spoke to her. He stopped in the middle of His time away, listened to her, thought about what she was saying, and replied. What a wonderful picture of God's character when it comes to the times we bring Him our problems! God loves us that much!

197

This love can be traced all the way back to the beginning. In Genesis 1:27 we hear, *"So God created man in his own image, in the image of God he created him; male and female he created them."* Much has been written about the image of God. Scholars have said this phrase means we were created with a rational soul. They've said it means we were created with moral discernment. Those interpretations may very well be true. Some scholars say the image of God was holiness and it was lost after the fall into sin. I'm not so sure about that one. In fact, I am convinced there is another more wonderful teaching in this Biblical phrase, "the image of God." I'm convinced it is a great statement of God's love for you.

Genesis 9:6 says the image of God still applies to us even after the fall into sin. God instructed Noah: *"Whoever sheds the blood of man, by man shall his blood be shed; for in the image of God has God made man."* Even in the New Testament we are described as being in the image of God. Paul gave worship instructions in 1 Corinthians 11:7, *"A man ought not to cover his head, since he is the image and glory of God."* What is significant about this Biblical description of us human beings? The word for "image" is a Hebrew word that referred to idols. They were things that people loved, trusted and worshipped. Leviticus 26:1 is a good example: *"Do not make idols or set up an image or a sacred stone for yourselves, and do not place a carved stone in your land to bow down before it."* The word for "image" in that verse refers to an idol. It is what was loved more than anything else in the people's lives.

Fast-forward to the New Testament. We see that Jesus is referred to as the "image of God." 2 Corinthians 4:4 says, *"The god of this age has blinded the minds of unbelievers, so that they cannot see the light of the gospel of the glory of Christ, who is the image of God."* Colossians 1:15 declares: *"[The Son of God] is the image of the invisible God, the firstborn over all creation."* What are these verses getting at? Are the New Testament passages telling us that Jesus has a rational soul? That He has moral discernment? Aren't they telling us that Jesus is God the Father's image—that which He loves more than anything else? God said it more than once about His Son, *"This is my Son, whom I love" (Matthew 3:17).* Aren't these passages that refer to Jesus as the "image of God" telling us there was an incredible relationship between the Father and the Son? There was oneness. There was unity. There was perfect love.

Here's the point about you and me: If the word "image" refers to what a person loves more than anything else, and if the phrase "image of God" refers to what God loves more than anything else, isn't the statement that we were created in the image of God pointing us to God's immeasurable love for us? You might say that God "worships the ground we walk on"! He treasures us above all of His creation. He's crazy about us. He created us in an incredible relationship with Him, and He sent His Son to redeem that relationship. Why? He loves us.

That's why Jesus didn't run out on the Canaanite woman. He loved her. That's why God doesn't groan when you bring your problems to Him, when you beg Him for help, when you pester Him about your latest worries and concerns. He

199

"idolizes" you! That's why you're totally wrong if you think you're a second class person compared to all the first-class people out there. When you believe that, you're insulting God. God loves you! There is only one reason to choose a bride—love. You have been chosen as the bride of Christ! What does that mean? God loves you!

GOD'S CHARACTER AND THE SENSIBILITY OF OUR ACTION

The third point this encounter makes clear deals with God's character and the sensibility of our action. The woman fell at Jesus' feet, worshipped Him and said, *"Lord, help me!"* Would Jesus respond? In other words, even though the plan is laid out, does God change? Does God really listen? Was this an exercise of frustration for the woman?

In order to answer these questions, let's take a look at one of the classic appeals for God's help. In Genesis 18 Abraham had an interesting dialog with God. God spoke to Abraham and revealed His plan to destroy Sodom. That's when the conversation started:

> *Then Abraham approached him and said: "Will you sweep away the righteous with the wicked? What if there are fifty righteous people in the city? Will you really sweep it away and not spare the place for the sake of the fifty righteous people in it? Far be it from you to do such a thing--to kill the righteous with the wicked, treating the righteous and the wicked alike. Far be it from you! Will not the Judge of all the earth do*

right?" The LORD said, "If I find fifty righteous people in the city of Sodom, I will spare the whole place for their sake." Then Abraham spoke up again: "Now that I have been so bold as to speak to the Lord, though I am nothing but dust and ashes, what if the number of the righteous is five less than fifty? Will you destroy the whole city because of five people?" "If I find forty-five there," he said, "I will not destroy it." Once again he spoke to him, "What if only forty are found there?" He said, "For the sake of forty, I will not do it." Then he said, "May the Lord not be angry, but let me speak. What if only thirty can be found there?" He answered, "I will not do it if I find thirty there." Abraham said, "Now that I have been so bold as to speak to the Lord, what if only twenty can be found there?" He said, "For the sake of twenty, I will not destroy it." Then he said, "May the Lord not be angry, but let me speak just once more. What if only ten can be found there?" He answered, "For the sake of ten, I will not destroy it." When the LORD had finished speaking with Abraham, he left, and Abraham returned home.

This conversation was as risky as the Canaanite woman's conversation with Jesus. It wasn't very dignified. Actually, it seemed a little embarrassing—old man Abraham calling into question God's flawless and righteous plan.

What was that conversation all about? It gives answers to the questions above. **Question 1: Does God change?** Answer: God is immutable, not inflexible. What does the word "immutable" mean? It means unchanging. So I am saying that God is unchanging, yet changing. Let me explain.

You may have read the Bible verses that talk about God being unchanging: Malachi 3:6, *"I the LORD do not change. So you, O descendants of Jacob, are not destroyed."* James 1:17, *"Every good and perfect gift is from above, coming down from the Father of the heavenly lights, who does not change like shifting shadows."* Hebrews 13:8, *"Jesus Christ is the same yesterday and today and forever."* There are more passages, but I think you get the idea. The Bible says that God doesn't change. This teaching is called the immutability of God.

On the other hand, God DOES change! You saw what happened in Genesis 18. God was going to destroy Sodom and Gomorrah. Abraham convinced God to change His criteria for destruction. In Exodus 32 God was ready to destroy the people of Israel because they were grumbling and worshiping a false god. Then Moses stepped in. Take a look at what happened:

> *But Moses sought the favor of the LORD his God. "O LORD," he said, "why should your anger burn against your people, whom you brought out of Egypt with great power and a mighty hand? Why should the Egyptians say, 'It was with evil intent that he brought them out, to kill them in the mountains and to wipe them off the face of the earth'? Turn from your fierce anger; relent and do not bring disaster on your people. Remember your servants Abraham, Isaac and Israel, to whom you swore by your own self: 'I will make your descendants as*

numerous as the stars in the sky and I will give your descendants all this land I promised them, and it will be their inheritance forever.'" Then the LORD relented and did not bring on his people the disaster he had threatened (Ex.32:11-14).

God changed. He relented. He wasn't just playing games with Moses. He actually heard Moses' request and had a change of heart.

What does all this mean? First, it means that God IS unchanging. The verses from Malachi and James make it clear that God is not two-faced. He does not have two different sides that He will flip around on you unpredictably. No, He is consistent. He has only one way of conducting Himself. And that way is a way of faithfulness. He will always be faithful. That is His nature. One of the Greek words in James for "does not change" is where we get our word "parallel" from. It's saying that God is not like parallel lines—one side for one moment, then the alternative the next moment, flipping from one track to the other. Hebrews 13:8 actually says that Jesus is HIMSELF, yesterday, today and into eternity. What you see is what you get. That's the way God is. Unchanging in His faithfulness.

On the other hand, God DOES change—not in His nature, but in His responsive heart. When it says in Exodus 32, "God relented"—in fact, in all the verses that say God "repented" (that's the way the King James Version phrases it), or changed His mind—the Hebrew word used means that God's heart was grieved. He felt compassion. He had a change of heart. His nature didn't change. In fact, this change of heart is consistent with His nature! God heard the appeal of His people and He responded.

That's what God does. Over and over in the Bible you can find verses like this one from Psalm 116: *"I love the LORD, for he heard my voice; he heard my cry for mercy" (vs.1).* God is unchanging, yet changing. He is immutable, but not inflexible.

Question 2: Does God really listen? Answer: God is your listener as well as your Lord. Everybody needs a listener. You need a listener, don't you? We show it all the time. When someone says to you, "I just went on the most amazing trip to Niagara Falls. It was so beautiful", what is the first way you feel like responding? Too often, the first thing you want to do is not ask some questions about the person's experience. Frequently, your gut reaction isn't to start finding out what their favorite site was, or where they stayed. You know what you feel like doing, don't you? You say: "I've been there too! Isn't it cool?" Or you say, "I had a great vacation this year, too!" Or, "I know someone who went there and almost fell right over the edge!" Then you start to tell *your* story!

What do you feel like doing when anyone talks about anything? You feel like talking about yourself. Why? Because you need a listener. Of course, it's very important to learn how to listen to others, but it's also important to know that you really need someone to listen to you. If you don't have anyone who takes an interest in you, your life feels very lonely and empty. One reason you fall in love with another person is because that person listens to you. One reason relationships break up is because people stop listening to each other. One strength of being in a small group at church or in your neighborhood is that you are gathered with people who will listen to you. Everybody needs a listener.

In Genesis 18 God showed that He is a listener. Let's review what God did: *Abraham remained standing before the LORD. Then Abraham approached him*—see? He was able to approach God—*and said: "Will you sweep away the righteous with the wicked? What if there are fifty righteous people in the city? Will you really sweep it away and not spare the place for the sake of the fifty righteous people in it? Far be it from you to do such a thing--to kill the righteous with the wicked, treating the righteous and the wicked alike. Far be it from you! Will not the Judge of all the earth do right?" The LORD said, "If I find fifty righteous people in the city of Sodom, I will spare the whole place for their sake."*

Abraham whittled the number down to 40 and continued: *Then he said, "May the Lord not be angry, but let me speak*—note that God let him speak! *What if only thirty can be found there?" He answered, "I will not do it if I find thirty there."*

Then down to 20 and the last request: *Then he said, "May the Lord not be angry, but let me speak just once more*—and what did God do? He listened. He listened to Abraham. *What if only ten can be found there?" He answered, "For the sake of ten, I will not destroy it."*

205

God listens to you. He will not change in His faithful attentiveness to you. He will hear the requests you offer. In Luke 18 Jesus told the parable of the widow and the unjust judge to teach His disciples that they should pray and not give up. You have a listener!

God even hears what you can't say. Romans 8:26 says that the Holy Spirit *"intercedes for us with groans that words cannot express."* God listens to the yearnings of your heart and soul. As He heard the blood of Abel cry out from the ground (Gen.4:10), He hears the cry of your life broken by sin and separation from Him. He hears your need to be made whole, to be restored, to be lifted up, to be loved. That is the need Abraham articulated to God when he was pleading for Sodom and Gomorrah. In verse 24 Abraham asked, "Will you not spare the place for the sake of 50 righteous people?" Literally the phrase is, "Will you not take up (or carry) this place?"—as in the sin and burden of this place. In some Bibles the word is translated "forgive." Abraham was focusing on our deepest need. He was saying, "Okay God, will you listen to THIS? Will you take up this, the greatest need ever?"

And God responded, "Yes I will! I will! I will take all those needs, all those sins, all those burdens!" And the ultimate demonstration of God taking up our brokenness is in Isaiah 53:4. The reference is to Jesus: *"Surely he **took up** our infirmities and carried our sorrows, yet we considered him stricken by God, smitten by him, and afflicted."* God did it! He answered Abraham's cry and the cry of your heart once and for all in Jesus! Do you see how God listens to you? He hears your every cry, your every word. Nothing will change that. In your deepest need God heard you and responded through His one and only Son who "was pierced for our transgressions…, crushed for our iniquities; the punishment that brought us peace was upon him, and by his wounds we are healed."

Question 3: Was this an exercise of frustration for the woman? Answer: No. This prayer was about faith, not frustration. Here's what I mean. Why did Abraham have to go through the drawn out process of bargaining with God? God knew his thoughts. Why didn't God give him the bottom line arrangement and then let the story unfold? God tells us why in Genesis 18:19. God said, *"For I have chosen [Abraham], so that he will direct his children and his household after him to keep the way of the LORD by doing what is right and just, so that the LORD will bring about for Abraham what he has promised him."* God was saying, "This is my guy. He is going to teach the future generations all about me. He is going to be so passionate about how faithful I am that he will live and breathe this message. Everyone in his family will be overwhelmed with his passionate witness about my love and justice and compassion."

So, what happened next? Abraham was put in the position of discovering God's love, justice and compassion. Abraham had to engage God in conversation. He had to test God. You heard him: *"Far be it from you to do such a thing--to kill the righteous with the wicked, treating the righteous and the wicked alike. Far be it from you! Will not the Judge of all the earth do right?"* These are the same words God focused on in verse 19—the righteousness and justice of God. This whole

207

conversation was about faith, not frustration. God was building Abraham's faith, his trust in and certainty of what God was really all about. It's significant that verse 33 says that Abraham returned home. Why did he go home? He went home to start telling his family about how faithful God is. Abraham grew in faith! Can you picture him opening the tent flap, walking in, sitting down for dinner and saying, "You'll never believe the conversation I just had with God. He totally cares."?

And that's the big question Jesus had in Luke 18. After He told the story of the widow and the unjust judge Jesus asked, *"When the Son of Man comes, will he find faith on the earth?"* In other words, God is faithful. He won't change. Will YOU have faith in Him? Will you keep talking to Him even when it SEEMS like He isn't listening? Will you still passionately trust that God's faithfulness and love for your life will not change? Will you grow in faith and not give up in frustration? God never changes. Your conversations with Him, your dialogue, and your struggles grow you to see that and to believe that.

That's exactly the pronouncement Jesus made about the Canaanite woman in Matthew 15. He said about the woman in verse 28, *"Woman, you have great faith!"* This work of Jesus would be contagious. The kingdom would be served. This encounter was about faith, not frustration. This encounter reveals the character of God and sheds light on the sensibility of our action.

WRESTLING WITH GOD

After the Canaanite woman's appeal for help, Jesus answered her, *"It is not right to take the children's bread and toss it to their dogs."* The woman responded, *"Yes, Lord, but even the dogs eat the crumbs that fall from their masters' table"* *(vss.26-27).*

Jesus wasn't insulting the woman. As He reinforced God's plan to the disciples, He also spelled out the plan for the woman. First the kids got the food. The pet dog got fed second. If you gave the pet all the food first, it wouldn't be right. It would actually be neglect!

But the woman ran with the analogy. She knew what it was like to have pets you love. She told Jesus that even the pets get the scraps while their masters are eating. Even Fido gets a few treats under the table! Notice that the woman respected God's plan. She called the people eating at the table "masters." They were entitled to the food, the woman said. God's plan and order is right and good. But then the woman went on to appeal to the love of Jesus, to the mercy of God. She was wrestling with God—and Jesus loved it!

Do you remember how Jacob wrestled with God? In Genesis 32 Jacob faced a stressful reunion with his estranged brother Esau. Jacob went to sleep on the evening before the meeting. That's when the wrestling match started. It went like this:

So Jacob was left alone, and a man wrestled with him till daybreak. When the man saw that he could not overpower him, he touched the socket of Jacob's hip so that his hip was wrenched as he wrestled with the man. Then the man said, "Let me go, for it is daybreak." But Jacob replied, "I will not let you go unless you bless me." The man asked him, "What is your name?" "Jacob," he answered. Then the man said, "Your name will no longer be Jacob, but Israel, because you have struggled with God and with men and have overcome" (vss.24-28).

Jacob refused to let God go until he received God's blessing. So God re-named Jacob "Israel." The name means "he wrestles with God." Think about it: the identity God gave His people, the name that indicated their character, the label that defined their being was "Israel." If you're one of God's people, you wrestle with Him. You contend. You ask questions. You talk with Him. You challenge Him. You bring Him your problems. The precise action Satan tries to cover up, God makes the name badge for His people!

Are you wrestling with God or are you staying out of the ring? Are you asking Him questions and bringing Him your problems or are you staying out of the fray? Are you taking a chance with God or are you giving up? God wants His people in the game, in the match! God wants His people to say, *"I will not let you go unless you bless me."* In the middle of trial, in the middle of things that don't make sense, in the middle of injustice, in the middle of questions, God wants you to hang on

210

to Him until you receive His blessing. That is what a lifetime of faith is all about. It's not a detached intellectual pursuit. It's not a quest for accumulating knowledge. It's not a blind and ignorant following. It is a wrestling match! That is what thrilled Jesus about the Canaanite woman. She hung on until she received the blessing of God.

HOW DOES GOD HELP YOU WITH YOUR PROBLEMS?

We hear the outcome of Jesus' encounter with the Canaanite woman in Matthew 15:28, *"Then Jesus answered, 'Woman, you have great faith! Your request is granted.' And her daughter was healed from that very hour."* What a great ending! The daughter was healed. The woman was relieved. Another kingdom victory happened. But what about you? What about the needs you have that haven't been completely solved? Is God brushing you off? Is Satan right about at least SOME of your problems?

This brings up an important question that needs answering: How does God help you with your problems? For the answer let's look at an incident in my life and an incident in Elijah's life.

A few months before I started writing this book I was in a harrowing car accident. As I merged onto the expressway near my house, a maroon GMC minivan traveling in the right lane moved reluctantly into the center lane to let me in. After I started to get into the flow of traffic, the van swerved sharply at me, running me off the road. The witness behind me said it looked like he did it on purpose. I avoided contact with his van, but, traveling at about 55 miles per hour, my car went into a series of 45 degree angle skids as I tried to regain control. Suddenly, the car grabbed the pavement and slammed head-on into a guardrail. The airbag didn't deploy, but the car bounced backwards into oncoming traffic, did a 360 degree turn, and slowed to a crawl facing the right direction. I was then able to coast out of the traffic lanes onto the shoulder of the road.

Miraculously, no one hit me when I bounced back into the roadway. The culprit in the van kept going (little did he know he would make it into print!). But a witness stopped to see if I was alright. My wife was able to come to the scene and drive me to the hospital. My car was towed away.

What I got out of the accident was some bruises, a case of whiplash, about $4000 worth of damage to my car, and an illustration for this book that I would not pass up! I also saw, very vividly, how God helps with our problems.

Where was God's help when the malicious van driver succeeded in running me off the road? What about all the other accidents and disasters that take place in your community and all around the world? What about countless numbers of people on this earth who are suffering? Victims of brutal murders, people hurting from chronic illness, and loved ones dying of cancer all could use God's help. But where is it? You go through tragedy, heartbreak and difficulty. Violence too awful for words rages in the lives of all people—rich and poor, adults and children. Where is God's help? Even Elijah, the prophet of God I mentioned above and previously in this book, experienced terrible threats, violence, fear, persecution and misery. Does God really help with our problems?

If He doesn't, He's worthless, isn't He? Because it is very evident that help is what we need. You don't have to be a Christian to come to the conclusion that life is a mess, that it can cause deep hurt on many levels, and that we need help in our brokenness. The Bible acknowledges that knowing what is right and wrong is written on our hearts. Deep inside, all of us face the brutal fact that we are flawed, broken—even devious, and headed toward death. So the question is, "Does God really provide help?" This is a serious question. If the answer is no, we have to fend for ourselves. If the answer is yes, we've got to learn how to recognize it.

And that brings me back to the car accident I had. Did God provide help for my problem? Let me share with you three ways I noticed God's provision of help.

First, I noticed what I'll call **preventing** help. The disastrous possibilities in that accident are too many to count. One change of direction and I could have hit the edge of the guardrail head-on. One change in the traffic pattern and an eighteen-wheeler two cars back would have surely flattened my little VW Beetle. And what odds would you give a car that bounced backwards into traffic on a busy Chicago expressway? I have no doubt in my mind that God was providing help. He and His angels were **preventing** disaster. You and I don't even realize all the things God prevents in order to keep our lives going! So, first, I noticed God's **preventing** help.

Second, I noticed what I'll call His **assisting** help. A woman by the name of Carol pulled over to the side, checked to see if I was alright, and waited with me for over an hour as the police came and got her account of what took place. She could have kept going to her job. I'm sure she was late for some important task at work. Who in a busy suburban area has time to stop everything for someone they don't even know— especially a woman stopping for a man during these violent and dangerous days? But Carol was God's **assisting** help for me. She heard His call, made the effort, and sacrificed what was happening in her life. God may not prevent all hurt, but He may **assist** in hurt.

Third, I noticed what I'll call God's **life-giving** help. As I crashed into the guard rail, bounced back into traffic, spun around, and braced myself for a high speed impact, was I afraid? When I managed to get to the side of the road, did I collapse in fear and anxiety because I could have died? No. Why? Because of God's **life-giving** help. I've got a home in heaven. The ultimate help God gives is that even though all of us will die one day, He broke the bonds of death through the death and resurrection of Jesus, His only Son. I don't want to die yet. I love my family, and I believe that God has a lot for me to do. But in this unfair and unpredictable world that is groaning in sin, death may come. It may hurt. It may be frightening. However, as the verse from Hebrews says, *"The Lord is my helper; I will not be afraid. What can man do to me?"*

214

(Hebrews 13:6) In Jesus Christ, God gives the ultimate help. I sensed that help very clearly as I crashed my car on the expressway. It was God's **life-giving** help.

But was this only my personal experience—all this help from God? Or is this a pattern of God's work among all of us? For the answer, listen to what happened in Elijah's life.

First, he experienced God's **preventing** help. He was delivered from King Ahab's wrath. He was protected from Queen Jezebel's threats. Time and again Elijah's demise was prevented by God's very evident intervention. God's **preventing** help was at work!

Second, Elijah experienced God's **assisting** help. 1 Kings 19:19 says, *"Elijah went from there and found Elisha son of Shaphat. He was plowing with twelve yoke of oxen, and he himself was driving the twelfth pair. Elijah went up to him and threw his cloak around him."* This was God's call to Elisha. The cloak, or mantle, was not only a sign that he was being called by God, but it passed on the Spirit of God that had filled Elijah. Like Carol on the expressway, Elisha was called by the Spirit and filled with the Spirit to give **assistance**. Verse 20 goes on to say, *"Elisha then left his oxen and ran after Elijah."* Elisha made an effort to follow God. When he asked to kiss his mom and dad good-bye (vs.20), it was not a case of hesitance. It was a demonstration that he meant business. When Elijah replied, *"Go back, what have I done to you?"* he was not being mean to Elisha. He was letting Elisha know that he could do what he needed to do in order to serve. Like Carol on the expressway,

215

Elisha suspended his busy schedule and made the effort to help. Verse 21 says Elisha *"took his yoke of oxen and slaughtered them. He burned the plowing equipment to cook the meat and gave it to the people, and they ate. Then he set out to follow Elijah and became his attendant."* Elisha sacrificed what was his to provide help—just like my helper, Carol. This was God's **assisting** help through Elisha. He heard God's call, made the effort, and sacrificed what was happening in his life. God didn't prevent all the hurt in Elijah's life, but He did **assist** in the hurt.

Third, God provided **life-giving** help. We hear in 2 Kings chapter two that Elijah knew that God was going to take him to heaven. The foundation of Elijah's life was the ultimate help: the **life-giving** help of God. I don't think it's any accident that we are told who appeared with Jesus on the mount of transfiguration in the Gospels. In Matthew 17 we read that as Jesus was transfigured before His disciples, and as they saw His glory as the true God, *"there appeared before them Moses and Elijah, talking with Jesus" (vs.3).* Elijah was talking with Jesus like an old friend. Elijah was alive and well. Elijah was living the eternal life God promised. God's **life-giving** help was very real!

So, God provided help for Elijah. He provided help for me. He provided help for the Canaanite woman. What about you? When you feel burned out and battered like Elijah, when you feel like you're spinning out of control and crashing like I was, when you feel like there may be no hope like the woman in Matthew 15 did, does God really help you with your problems? If He does, how can you spot it?

To explain, I would like you to think about a baseball bat. When I was a kid we always played baseball in my neighborhood. In order to pick teams, one captain would toss a bat to another captain and they would begin to place their hands on the bat, hand over hand. The person whose hand got to the nub of the handle first would be the person with the first pick.

This is a good illustration of what happens in your life. Jesus said in John 14:27, *"Peace I leave with you; my peace I give you. I do not give to you as the world gives. Do not let your hearts be troubled and do not be afraid."* So, the world gives one thing, but Jesus gives something else. Up the bat the hands go:

- The world gives disasters and tragedies; Jesus says, *"My peace I leave with you."*

- The world gives wars and the disruption and fear of loved ones called into service; Jesus says, *"I am with you always."*

- The world gives the fear of terrorist attacks; Jesus says, *"Do not let your hearts be troubled and do not be afraid."*

- The world gives awful television violence and sexual carelessness; Jesus says, *"Blessed are the pure in heart, for they will see God."*

- The world gives unemployment and economic woes; Jesus says, *"Do not worry, saying, 'What shall we eat?' or 'What shall we drink?' or 'What shall we wear?' For the pagans run after all these things, and your heavenly Father knows that you need them."*

- The world gives road rage and so much that takes life out of you; Jesus says, *"Take and eat, this is my body and this is my blood given for you."*

Up you go, back and forth. The world gives trouble, but God provides help—very real help. He provides **preventing** help in so many cases. He provides **assisting** help so many times. He provides a mix of the two, sometimes very evident, sometimes very subtle. Trouble, then God's help. Trouble, then God's help. Take a look and see if you can spot that as the pattern in your life!

But then the devil, the world, and our flesh try to make the final effort to destroy you. Illness, harm and death come your way. What's left? There's no room on the bat once you've reached that nub on the handle, is there? Well, if you've played baseball and picked teams with a bat, you know the secret weapon! At the last moment, when all hope is lost, there is the trump card! The bottlecap! That's what my friends and I used to do. We'd clamp our fingers around that little nub at the end of the bat handle and we'd say, "Bottlecaps!" That would give us first pick. That would give us the win. And that's exactly what Jesus does. Even in the face of all lost hope, Jesus says, "Bottlecaps! Ha! I am the resurrection and the life! Even though you die, yet you shall live!" (John 11:25) The death and resurrection of Jesus for you is God's **life-giving** help. Even if this world does you in, you still live! Even if **preventing** help and **assisting** help don't do the job, **life-giving** help from God never fails! It's the ultimate help, the solid foundation of your life. It's the most important help you could ever receive. The helpless Jesus on the cross didn't want you to ride only on the **preventing** and **assisting** help of God. He wanted you to have his **life-giving** help for all eternity. "Bring on those problems!" God says, "I've got more help than you can imagine!"

Do you see why Satan wants to keep you from bringing your problems to God? Your life is on the line! That's why the big question that permeates this lie of Satan is not whether God really wants to hear your problems; it is whether you will truly receive His help—all of it.

If you do, like the Canaanite woman, you will be surprised and delighted. I was surprised the day I was putting this portion of the chapter together. I happened to glance at the notes I made from my insurance company after the accident happened. On those notes I wrote this name: "Elisha." I thought, "Elisha? Why did I write that? I wasn't even thinking about Elisha then." Then I remembered. The name of the kind claims contact person from my insurance company was Elisha (pronounced Eleesha). Well wasn't that amazing? Elijah and I had something in common that fateful week. With a sense of humor and with poignancy, God really does help us with our problems. He wants to be bothered!

Satan's Lies
Your Actions

Lie #14: "You're Better Off On Your Own"

_____

GOING IT ALONE?

"Master," said John, "we saw a man driving out demons in your name and we tried to stop him, because he is not one of us."

"Do not stop him," Jesus said, "for whoever is not against you is for you" (Luke 9:49-50).

John had just experienced the thrill of Jesus' transfiguration. He was riding high about his insider status with Jesus. The other disciples were feeling the same way. They were just discussing who was the greatest. These guys were feeling like the elite, exclusive, privileged set. So, when they saw someone who was "not one of us" casting out demons, they put a stop to it. They wanted to go it alone. And once again, Satan cheered.

"You're better off on your own!" Satan says. "After all, if you want to get something done, do it yourself." "Too many cooks spoil the soup. Why bother with getting other people involved?" "God helps those who help themselves. Do it yourself, THEN you can ask God for His input."

Yes, Satan says all those things. And they're all lies. He wants to isolate you. He wants to lead you to rely on your own strength. He wants to separate you from other people and God. But what's the truth?

Over the years I've found it helpful to be attentive to people who have walked the road of life before me. When I was a kid I worked for some older gentlemen—both were in their seventies and eighties. They were born around 1900. August Rosenwinkel and Reinhard Eikelmann showed me the value of listening to the voices of experience. They wowed me with stories of highway robbers, the World Wars, movie stars who passed through Chicago, the early days of airplane travel, and lots more. I was glad to get a paycheck when I worked with them, but what I looked forward to most was their stories. Those men were instrumental in making me attentive to experienced people. And when you are eager to hear people talk, you never know who you might encounter.

MY WEATHERMAN IDOL

About six months before I started writing this book, I had the opportunity to listen to the weatherman who I watched on TV all the years I was growing up. His name is Harry Volkmann. I actually had the chance to sit at the feet of my weatherman idol! Harry Volkmann started doing Chicago weather for NBC in 1959. Through the years he made moves to WGN, CBS, and, at the time I heard him, he was forecasting the weather on our local Fox channel. I thought Harry Volkmann was great! I always enjoyed watching him give weather reports and predictions when I was a kid, and I was thrilled about his continued work. Now, there he was—right before my eyes!

How did this meeting happen? Harry has always made the rounds speaking to various groups. Every time he was doing the weather he was wearing a special boutonniere from a group he spoke to that day. He always announced the group and said hello on the air. Well, I happened to be visiting a wonderful lady in a local retirement center. We finished a short devotion with communion when I heard over the loudspeaker that Harry Volkmann was coming to visit. I said to her, "Do you want to go? We've got to see Harry if he's here." She agreed—perhaps humoring the pastor who was so excited about seeing a TV weatherman.

We went down to the meeting room. It was filled with people eager to see the man who forecast 2-3 inches of snow on the fateful day of one of the biggest blizzards in the Chicago area. That was back in January of 1967. Chicago ended up getting 23 inches of snow! Harry said that it was just a matter of punctuation. He should have taken that dash out of the 2-3. He was close, he said!

So there I was in the front row listening to Harry Volkmann. And when Harry started to talk to the group, what a surprise it was to hear his voice of experience talking about the fact that you're never better off on your own.

Harry talked about his mother. She had a hard life. Her husband, Harry's dad, died in the military around the time of

World War One. Harry never knew him. So mom lived as a single mother in those early days of the 1900's. In fact, she never remarried. Harry Volkmann's mother was a widow for 60 years.   How did she make it through her loneliness and heartbreak?   How did she handle it when she was so overwhelmed with financial needs, work demands, and the pressure of being both mom and dad? Harry made it clear that his mom didn't go it alone.

Harry's mom was an immigrant from Germany. She began to work as an English teacher—helping other immigrants learn the language. She was so proud to be in this country she also taught citizenship classes so other immigrants could become official members of the United States. Seeing the need for a voice in the decision making process of this country, Harry's mom became a suffragette—a woman who campaigned for the privilege of voting. She wasn't a bra-burning militant, Harry said, but she worked hard for a constitutional amendment that would allow women to vote. How do you think Harry's mom made it through as she faced discrimination, insult and opposition?   How did she survive when work became frustrating, when people didn't respond, when she felt left out? Harry made it clear that his mom didn't go it alone.

It wasn't long before Harry was called to serve in the military. World War Two was upon our country and Harry became an artilleryman stationed in Germany. Can you imagine what awful memories and feelings of loss this brought up? Mrs. Volkmann's husband was lost in one war. What would happen to her son?   How did Mrs. Volkmann make it through that worry, stress and strain? How can anyone make it when they face an unknown future, an unforeseen development in life, danger and violence, and a loved one in the thick of it? Harry made it clear that his mom didn't go it alone.

NEVER ON HER OWN

Harry Volkmann's mom taught him that you're never better off on your own. Even though she was left as a single mom to face insurmountable odds during her day and age, she showed her son that walking with God and with His people was the only way to make it through. As I listened to my favorite weatherman, I was thrilled to hear him give witness to another kind of climate, the climate of his soul. He said that throughout his lifetime, he too found peace and strength with His Lord Jesus. For his mother and for himself, Jesus was there all along.

This was a great voice of experience to hear. It was a double voice. Harry and his mother were giving witness to the presence of Jesus. As I listened I could tell that this was a passion Mrs. Volkmann instilled in her son. This had nothing to do with personal strength or positive thinking. This was a clear endorsement of the personal presence of Jesus. Harry made the strong point: you're never better off on your own. His mom knew it. He knew it too.

That's what Jesus was telling John and the other disciples in Luke chapter nine. He said, *"Do not stop him, for whoever is not against you is for you" (vs.50).* Jesus let His followers know that work for the kingdom was not a solo act.

Life itself was not a solo act. Going through life was not about selfishness and control. It was about serving together.

Paul said in 1 Corinthians 12, *"The body is a unit, though it is made up of many parts; and though all its parts are many, they form one body. So it is with Christ. For we were all baptized by one Spirit into one body--whether Jews or Greeks, slave or free--and we were all given the one Spirit to drink. Now the body is not made up of one part but of many" (vss.12-14).* Paul went on to describe how the body works together—how each part doesn't insist on being on its own. He summed up this analogy in verse 27 when he said, *"Now you are the body of Christ, and each one of you is a part of it."*

How many times do you start to think of yourself as the center of the universe? Your ministry, your success in a career, your knowledge, your problems, your goals—they're all you think about. When someone begins a conversation, do you always bring it around to yourself—what you're doing, what you're thinking, what you've accomplished? Do you realize you're part of a big picture? Who you are is important, but you're not the self-sufficient solo act. God is using you for crucial work in this world, but you need Him and you need the other people of this world to accomplish the bigger plan—God's plan.

Jesus was telling His disciples: "There's more than just you." Paul was telling believers: "You need each other and you need Christ, the head of the body." Harry Volkmann was telling us: "Going it alone would have never worked—for me or for my mom." Those authoritative voices of experience make a very good case against Satan's lie.

WALKING WITH JESUS

For sixty years of widowhood, Mrs. Volkmann knew and taught that the only way to get through life was with God—His Spirit with her, guarding her, standing by her, even when life was terrible and overwhelming.

Harry learned the same thing. He told the story of a time when he was a young boy in school and was asked by the teacher how to spell rhythm. Harry responded R-H-Y-T-H-M. Then the teacher asked the smartest kid in the class to spell rhythm. This guy was Mr. Popular. Everybody liked him. Everybody wanted to hang around him. The boy responded R-Y-T-H-M-N. A disagreement. So the teacher asked Harry and the other speller to stand up in front of the class. They did. Harry's heart was pounding. The teacher then asked all the students to come up front and stand with the person they thought spelled rhythm correctly. Every student gathered around the smartest kid in the class. Harry was left alone. The teacher looked at Harry and asked, "Harry, do you want to stand with everyone else?" Harry responded with a shaky voice, "No, ma'am, because then I would be spelling rhythm incorrectly." The teacher asked all the other kids to sit down. She announced, "Harry Volkmann, you spelled rhythm correctly. But there was something better you just did. You stood by your belief even under the pressure of every other student in this room."

Harry's mother taught him about that already. Even in adversity, even when everyone else is claiming to be right, even when the world is trying to push you in the wrong direction, there is One with you to keep you strong. Going it alone doesn't work when the pressure is on.

ARE YOU ALONE?

What about your life? Are you on your own? A little while back I read the results of a survey conducted in northwest suburban Chicago. It listed the top five challenges people were facing. Number one on the list was loneliness.

The devil is very tricky about this struggle. On one hand he tries to convince you that you should be self-sufficient, independent, relying on nobody. Then, on the other hand, he makes you feel like a loser because you don't have any close friends. The devil lures you into isolation, filling your head with thoughts like, "No one really understands me. Who would want to spend time with me, anyway? God isn't hearing my prayers." But, once you are isolated, the devil tortures you with feelings of loneliness and failure. In isolation, frequently he succeeds in luring people into hidden sins and addictions. Then he loads them up with guilt, driving them further and further away from God and others.

Do you feel alone? In Luke chapter nine, Jesus said He came to change that. Jesus let the disciples know He was here to spread His presence around. He was going to be with all His people, and He was going to make sure they walked through life as one.

How did Jesus make that happen? Let's call it "moving day." Into your isolation and loneliness, God declared it moving day. It happened on the day God's only Son hung from the cross. That was the day God closed the deal to move into your life. You were locked up, deadbolted, by sin and Satan. But in His suffering and death Jesus' made full payment for your life, and in His resurrection He took the house keys of your heart and soul so He could move right in. With you. Always. Never again on your own. Placed by grace into a new homeowner's association—God's people, His body, the church.

That's what the Bible says. In Ephesians two you hear, *"You were separate from Christ, excluded from citizenship in Israel and foreigners to the ...promise, without hope and without God...But now in Christ Jesus you who once were far away have been brought near through the blood of Christ. Consequently, you are no longer foreigners...but fellow citizens with God's people and members of God's household built on the foundation of the apostles and prophets, with Christ Jesus himself as the chief cornerstone...In him you too are being built together to become a dwelling in which God lives by his Spirit"* (vss.12-13, 19-20, 22).

Jesus said, *"I am with you always"* (Matthew 28:20) for a reason! He knew that you're never better off on your own. You need Him and all He gives.

Recently I met with a man who for many years had resisted having Christ in his life. He was struggling with major intellectual questions about the Bible and about faith. His life, however, had taken a turn for the worse. He lost a lot of money. He lost his job. There was uncertainty everywhere. That's when he let Jesus in. He told me, "I realized that I needed Jesus. Even for the intellectual struggles I realized that maybe I would find out more with Jesus than without him." He realized he was not better off on his own.

That's why Mrs. Volkmann could make it for so long through so much. That's why Harry Volkmann, TV weatherman, could give a witness at the retirement center. That's God's good message to you today.

BILL

Will you hear it? Will you really listen?

My tendency is to go it alone. I'm like a lot of people. Whether it's a home project or a ministry task, I tend to want to go solo. But I've been learning.

I served for fifteen years in an amazing church in which people wouldn't let anyone go it alone! When my wife was recovering from the severe illness in the early part of her pregnancy with our second daughter, I learned to say "thank you" as people brought meals to us and helped us in many ways. Sometimes you have to get to the point of being helpless before you recognize what a blessing NOT being on your own is.

Over twenty years ago I knew a young man by the name of Bill. We were friends and co-workers for a couple of years during high school. Bill was a great guy. He was the oldest son in a big Irish Catholic family. Bill studied hard and got good grades. He worked hard and made some good money. He was a nice kid.

Bill's youngest sister idolized him. She was only about seven years old, but she never missed a chance to give him a big hug and say, "Billy, I love you." She did it in front of everyone when she walked him into work. Bill was about six-foot-two, but he always bent down and got that big hug around the neck—even in front of us, his cool high school friends. He always stood up blushing as he watched his sister trot back out to his parents' car. I can still see Bill standing there in front of the timeclock; face all red, trying not to make eye contact with any of us. We never said anything. We just watched his little sister go skipping down the hall and out the door. I suppose there are certain things even a group of cool high school boys recognize as very important.

Bill's youngest sister was quite a character. She had the softest heart in the world—especially for God's creatures that might be in jeopardy. She fed the squirrels that lived around their family's old frame two story house. She brought neighborhood cats in to feed them snacks after school. She wanted to rescue every puppy in the pet shop. She even got in big trouble for taking the screen out of a window in an effort to coax a crow into her room. He looked cold, she said.

231

Almost every day she would give a report of her latest rescue efforts: "Look what I found," she would say, as she pointed to the latest cat in the house or as she lifted up the inchworm that she snatched from an evil spider's control. "Look what I found, Billy!"

We really got a kick out of Bill's little sister.

As time went on at work, I saw Bill's clear and blue eyes get bloodshot with drug use. It started with smoking pot. It moved into speed and cocaine and more. Drugs were offered to all of us, but Bill said yes. Another friend and I urged Bill to stop. But he wouldn't.

Over the period of one year I saw Bill's grades plummet, his hopes for a good college and a good scholarship crumble, and his relationship with his parents get thrown into disarray. Bill had a hollow and sad look. He wasn't the same. He was isolated, alone, at the lowest point he could be.

Apparently, that's when his sister stepped in. She wasn't able to give him those hugs around the neck much, lately. Their lack of closeness had bothered her for some time. One late afternoon when Bill wasn't working, his sister opened his bedroom door—a courageous thing to do at that time. Bill's heart was hard, but not too far gone at that point to show a little kindness to the sister who adored him. He asked her, "Where's your latest find?"

His sister looked into his empty eyes in the dim light of the room. "Can I find you?" she asked. "Can I find you?"

232

Bill's sister had a soft heart for God's creatures who might be in jeopardy. Her loving heart and her loving question did for Bill what none of us could do. His life started to change because his sister looked for him and asked if he would be found.

That's what Jesus asks you as you read this chapter. "Have you gone off on your own? Can I find you?" Satan is wrong. We're not better off on our own. We need Jesus and we need each other.

After Harry Volkmann spoke we shook his hand and thanked him. My friend and I made our way back to her room. We were in good spirits. And as I bid her farewell, I knew with even more certainty that in her room in the retirement center, right next to her wheelchair, through the effects of the stroke she had a while back, and for her heart that grieved the death of her husband, there was Jesus. She was not on her own. Neither was I. The forecast was a 100% chance of Christ's presence and help all the way to life everlasting.

Satan's Lies
Your Actions

Lie #15: "You Can't Really Change Who You Are"

CAN YOU EVER CHANGE?

I started to get worried when I realized the wonderful girl I met in college was the person I wanted to marry. I didn't worry because of anything about her. I worried because I felt my life was missing something. Would I be capable of sustaining a healthy marriage relationship? At that point in my life my parents were divorced. After years of struggles in their relationship, the marriage ended. I knew I hadn't received an ideal example of communication, conflict resolution, and overall management of a marriage relationship. My question was whether I would be able to do something different in the marriage I was headed toward. Was I shackled to dysfunctional behavior and bad habits? Could I change?

I remember the moment this panic took command of my heart. I was walking across my college campus—in the middle of a field as I headed to classes. The fear came out of nowhere. It hit hard. I could almost see the chains in my life that locked me in to past behavior and examples. Deep inside I wondered, "How could I ever know anything different?" The answer seemed to be that I never could.

The class I happened to be walking to was called "Marriage and the Family." The teacher happened to be my future father-in-law. He happened to be assigning a class project on one Biblical aspect of marriage. I happened to choose communication.

You've reached a point in this book where I hope you recognize spiritual warfare when you see it. The devil was assaulting me with doubt and fear. God was lining up a counter-attack of hope rooted in His Word of life. It's really amazing to look back on.

This may not only be my story, however. Perhaps you are feeling the way I felt. Maybe your life hasn't been the "ideal" life to live. Was your life at home messed up? Were you abused as a child or as an adult? Have you been trapped in addiction or dysfunction? Are you losing hope because of depression that plagues you? Have you failed in a marriage? Have you disappointed or hurt your kids? Do you feel shackled to your past? Do you wonder if there is any possible way you can live any differently?

The devil would tell you there isn't. In the same way he filled my mind and spirit with hopelessness and fear, he says to you, **"You can't really change who you are."** And you believe him. After all, with all that's gone on in your life, how can you figure out any way to change anything? I used to measure our home life against the "Brady Bunch" television show (what did I know?). I believed that because I had no examples of a healthy relationship, I could never know how to live in one. I thought that even if I managed to sustain a relationship, underneath the surface of my life would be all kinds of dysfunction ready to explode, ready to ruin everything. It was very frightening to be in a position with no tools, no resources, and no foundation. I knew I would fail. That might be how you feel as you read this.

I've got news for you: both of us are right. If it all was up to US, we would totally fail. This lie of Satan is a half-truth. YOU can't change who you are. I couldn't change the crumbling foundation I was given for marriage. But I found out who could.

I started my project for the "Marriage and the Family" class. My task was to search the Bible for its counsel about communication in marriage. That project opened my eyes. Over and over again I found words of God that supplied a foundation in life. I read about God's faithful communication with us. I read God's counsel and direction for husbands and wives. I read about self-sacrifice, speaking the truth in love, forgiving each other, and not going to bed mad (read the book of Ephesians if you want to get a good sampling of this!). I also saw that, as a member of God's family, I DID have a family that modeled this perfect love. God the Father and God the Son, Jesus my brother by grace, showed me everything perfectly. They did it all better than the Brady Bunch! Not only that, the Bible promised me that this foundation of new life was mine. In Christ I was a new creation. The old was gone. The new had come (2 Corinthians 5:17). As I completed my "Marriage and the Family" class project I could see the chains to the past being broken. I rejoiced in the opportunity to start a new history.

And that is what God gave me. As I write these lines, my wife and I are nearing twenty-five years of marriage. They've been years filled with God's grace and blessing. They've been years of learning and growth. They've been years of practicing self-sacrifice and living out what love really is. They've been great years! God does amazing things.

In 1 John 3:7 we hear, *"Children, let no one lead you astray. The one doing the right things of God is righteous, just as Jesus is righteous"* (my more literal translation). In Christ we receive the blessing of new life that not only impacts the mind and spirit, but also changes our actions, that radically transforms our life into a life like Jesus, a life saturated with His righteousness. Jesus really works. Does that mean you become perfect? No. But it means there is hope for broken lives. You have a chance to live the life Jesus earned for you at the cross. Your actions can be redeemed by Christ.

As I said, YOU can't change who you are. But there is One who can. With Jesus it's a different story! Consider this story of two men who saw how Jesus changes lives. I've changed the names of the main characters and adjusted a few details for the sake of confidentiality, but the story is true. It is a powerful testimony to the fact that God can change who you are.

NELS AND JOHN

They were 18 years old. They had no money. It was the post-depression 1930's. But they did have lots of fun. They saw some movies—even a few good ones. And girls. That was definitely one of their interests. Chicago was a bustling town with lots of opportunities for two red-blooded Americans. New Americans, that is. John was English. Nels was Norwegian. Both were born in their mother countries, but their parents moved to the U.S. It was the land of opportunity—even in hard times. These two young men were friends, joined at the hip. They talked sports, dreams, the future, and the past. They listened to each other's struggles, cares, worries and fears. They were friends, real friends.

As Christmas approached, Nels wondered about an appropriate Christmas gift for John. Nels had no money. That ruled out most of the list. But there was one thing. There was one precious thing he'd been wanting to give for a while. You see, John was a lost friend. He was energetic, fun, stubborn and filled with loads of English loyalty. But he was lost. He didn't know Jesus. He had no Savior. He possessed no hope. He had no deed to a home in heaven. He didn't even think about such an acquisition. He was going to die and be lost forever.

Nels talked to John about this before. Several times as a matter of fact. Not only was there no acceptance, there was opposition. At first it was lighthearted. Nels would tell John, "Jesus saves." John would answer, "Oh yeah? At what bank?" But then the opposition grew strong and serious. "Never bring that up again," John told Nels.

But it was 1938. Hitler was storming through Europe. Word was that military service would be coming. There may not be another Christmas for them. So, Nels decided to give it all, to give his best, the best gift he could think of, to his dearest friend. He would risk it all—risk being disliked, risk the present for the sake of eternity. He would try to give John the greatest gift—a Savior, Jesus, the gift of life from God.

WHAT NELS KNEW

Nels understood the mysterious power of the Gospel of Christ. 1 John 3:8 says, *"The reason the Son of God appeared was to destroy the devil's work."* We came across that verse in the beginning chapter of this book. The word for "destroy" in the verse literally means "to loose," "to leave behind." Think about that. Jesus came to cut loose the devil's work in your life. Jesus came to leave all the dysfunction, the sin, the doubt, the wrong examples—He came to leave it all behind. That means He came to change who you are, to give you a fresh start, to begin a new history in your life.

Of course, you may need to work with a counselor. You may need a psychiatrist's care and medication. You may need to work through difficult issues in your relationships. All of this may take a lot of time and effort. It may be something that lasts a lifetime. But do you see that all those things are open doors from Jesus? All those things mean that the devil's work can truly be left behind! It can be cut loose! You can have new life and new hope! Jesus changes who you are.

THE CHALLENGE TO BE CHANGED

"How about a movie?" Nels asked. A new western was playing. It was Nels' treat. John had no money and no options. "Of course, let's go," he replied.

The friends walked down the decorated Chicago streets. They could see the vapor from their breath forming wintry clouds and disappearing as they walked through them. The store windows seemed to spill over onto the sidewalks with gifts and decorations. Soot-covered snow lay piled along the curbs. Streetcars glided by as masses of people made their way in many directions along the same route. Nels looked around at all the people and thought about the gift he wanted to give.

"How will I bring this up?" he wondered to himself. He could see the theater ahead. It was time. He cleared his throat and fidgeted with his coat. John looked at him and said, "What's wrong with you?"

This was the cue. "The same thing that's wrong with you," Nels replied. "With you and everyone! Do you see it? Do you see it in yourself? You're poor. Your parents are ill. You're unable to go to school. You're unable to control your life. You're helpless, man! You've got no future!"

John cleared the shocked look from his face and answered wryly, "Thanks for the cheerful news, old boy."

Nels continued, "What I'm trying to say is that you need a gift this Christmas, John. You need Jesus! He died for your

241

miserable life. He died and rose to give you something to hope for. And He died 'cause He loves your ornery English self and wants you in heaven with Him. I want you there too. Will you wake up, stop your stubbornness and do something about it? This is my Christmas gift for you. Will you take it?

John looked him in the eye. He paused and walked away.

Nels sat down and wept. They didn't make it to the movie.

RIGHT AND WRONG

The apostle appealed in 1 John 3:7, *"Dear children, do not let anyone lead you astray."* There is a time to assess what is happening in your life. The verses go on to say, *"He who does what is right is righteous, just as he is righteous. He who does what is sinful is of the devil, because the devil has been sinning from the beginning" (vss.7-8).* The word for "sinful" in verse eight is rooted in the New Testament word for "witness" or "testimony." The Greek word for "sinful" attaches a negative to the word, making it "un-witness" or "false witness." The devil is all about untruth and bad testimonies. He steers you the wrong way. From the beginning his goal has been to get you on the wrong track.

Is that happening in your life? Are you living in untruth? Are you on the wrong track in your relationships, with your attitude, with your habits? Take a close look. As a pastor I have the opportunity to talk to a lot of people about their lives. One of the most frustrating experiences I have is to watch people nod in agreement when they hear the transforming Word of God, but live as if they never heard it! Some people are all for mission programs, all for church expansion, all for effectively functioning children's ministries and student ministries, but when it comes to assessing their own lives, they never get past church attendance. They go home and use foul language. They treat their wives with disrespect. They speak negatively and unkindly about others. Sometimes I feel like shouting, "Stop! Take a look at YOUR life—all of it. Do a thorough assessment. Are you being led astray? Where is Jesus leading you?" It can be painful to assess your life, but it's something you should do over and over again. Why? Because Jesus will change who you are.

LIFE ASSESSMENT

John went home. He was disgusted, mad, and frustrated. But his heart hurt. He got ready for bed and sat down on the edge of his mattress. Nels' words coursed through his thoughts. He sat for two hours. Two hours of thought about his life, who he was, where he was going, and what he needed. Finally John fell to his knees. Tears filled his eyes as he began a conversation he never ever had before:

> "He was right. That Norwegian was right. I've got nothing, and I'll end up with nothing—even if I get it all. God, I don't want my life to be a waste. I've got some big questions still. I'm not letting you off the hook. I don't understand why my parents are suffering so

much. I don't understand why times are so hard. I don't understand a lot. But I do know I need something. I need someone. I need help that's bigger than me. God, I'll take the gift. If you really want to give it to the likes of me, I'll take the gift."

And God gave it. That cold December night, God gave it. There was no earthquake, no audible angel song, no rumble of thunder or flicker of a burning bush. But the gift was given and received, and a life was new and changing.

AN AMAZING GIFT

You can't change who you are, but there is a Savior who gives you new birth. Remember when Nicodemus, the frightened church leader, came to Jesus at night in John chapter three? He inquired about this new thing Jesus was doing. Jesus said to him, *"I tell you the truth, no one can see the kingdom of God unless he is born again."* Nicodemus responded with the shock we would respond with: *"How can a man be born when he is old? Surely he cannot enter a second time into his mother's womb to be born!"* Then Jesus let Nicodemus know that while you can't change who you are, there is a gracious God who has opened the door to new life. Jesus said, *"I tell you the truth, no one can enter the kingdom of God unless he is born of water and the Spirit. Flesh gives birth to flesh, but the Spirit gives birth to spirit"* *(vss.3-6).* Nicodemus asked again, *"How can this be?"* And Jesus gave the greatest gift we could ever receive. He told Nicodemus and He tells us, *"God so loved the world that he gave his one and only Son, that whoever believes in him shall not perish but have eternal life" (vs.16).*

Life. What a stark contrast to the destruction of the devil. What a remarkable gift to have life now and forever through Jesus. The devil gives a false life, an empty wrapper. Jesus gives real life, life in all its fullness (John 10:10).

That's what happened to the John of our story that Christmas. He received life. There is no way to describe the rest of John's lifetime in the confines of a short chapter like this. But fast-forward sixty-three years. John sits at the bedside of a new friend. The man lost his wife to cancer. Now this poor soul was dying. He resisted John's attempts over the years—John's gift-giving attempts. But now this man saw death face-to-face. And he said to John, "Please pray for me."

John replied, "No. No, I won't. Unless I first can share the Gospel of Jesus with you."

"Please, yes," the friend said.

And John did. From the manger to the cross, to our look in the mirror, to the new life from a living Jesus, to a home in heaven. The dying friend received the gift that day. And John prayed for him.

The next day, the friend's son called. Dad had died, the son shared. "But I saw a profound change. He confessed faith in Jesus. He died with such peace," the son said.

John shared the gift he had received over sixty years ago. He shared it with joy and passion. The gift of God's love made a difference. If you had a time-line view of John's life since that day he and Nels were walking to the movie, you would see new, gift-filled lives all along the way. John's life was changed. Was his life an exception? Was it an oddity? Is it an impossible dream for you? Remember what Jesus said, *"With man this is impossible, but not with God; all things are possible with God"* *(Mark 10:27).*

I sat with the real John this year when he told me he made a Christmas phone call. He called Nels. He said to Nels, "Friend, I wanted to thank you for the best gift you could have ever given me—faith in my Lord Jesus Christ."

Yes, that Christmas two octogenarians rejoiced that Jesus can change who you are. Do you believe He can change you?

Satan's Lies
Conclusion

Lie #16: "You Can Forget About Me Now"

THE END

Congratulations! You've come to the end of this book. It's not a small feat. I suspect Satan may have been fighting you the whole way. I almost called this book "Spiritual Warfare and Other Major Household Appliances." Why? Because the warfare of the one whose time is short stops at nothing. If you're getting filled spiritually, the devil will do his all to distract and demoralize you. He'll throw in a broken garage door, a wash machine that overflows, a freezer that fails, a muffler that falls off the car, and more! Distraction. Inconvenience. Torment. I wouldn't be surprised if a few things broke down where you live while you have been reading this book.

You must understand that so often spiritual warfare happens in the little things. You've probably noticed it, but, perhaps, haven't realized what was going on. When the big trials come, you handle them. You pull together with family members when a loved one is ill or dies. The whole community rallies together when a major disaster happens. You seek professional help when there is a crisis with someone you care about.

But it's the little things that throw you for a loop! They sneak up on you, accumulate, and send you over the edge. The kids leave their shoes in the middle of the floor again, your husband leaves his underwear in the bathroom, the paper delivery person tosses the paper into the bush after you've asked to have it placed on the porch, the pastor preaches long again and you can't get to lunch on time, your co-worker keeps making a funny sound with her teeth in the cubicle next to you. And what is your response? After suffering too many annoyances, you lose it. Your spiritual demeanor goes out the window. Every lesson of faith is tossed aside as you let loose at the person who is the straw who breaks the camel's back.

And Satan laughs, "Gotcha!"

When I started to write this book I also kept a close watch for the devil's attacks in my life. I have a lot of brothers and sisters in Christ praying for me, so I know the Lord is giving strong protection. But I've seen Satan try to meddle. I've felt his attempts to trample me and to claim me as his turf. His fury has been noticeable. But God has been faithful. His strong defense can't be beat.

Now that you've read this book, you have increased your awareness about the battle that rages and about God's great work in your life. But the devil has one more trick up his sleeve. It's the last of Satan's lies I'm going to mention. Satan says, **"You can forget about me now."**

When you are finished with this book, you'll put it down and get on with your day to day living. Please realize that at every moment the devil will try to lull you into a false sense of security. He will do his all to let you live a normal and uneventful life, all the while loading you up for collapse. Remember, his goal is to destroy you, to pull you away from Jesus, and to make you forget about your purpose in God's kingdom.

But the devil does not have the last word. The Word made flesh has that! That's why Jesus came to this normal world and lived a normal life. It's the location of the battle. Remember, the dragon was "hurled to the earth" (Revelation 12:13). So Jesus went through it all. He had to help do the dishes. He experienced the frustration of sweeping up after the day was over only to have the wind blow all the dust back into the house. He hit His thumb a few times with the hammer when Joseph was teaching Him carpentry. He had customers complain that the job wasn't done right or on time. He had His favorite chisel give out in the middle of an important task. Referring to Jesus, Hebrews 4:15 says, *"For we do not have a high priest who is unable to sympathize with our weaknesses, but we have one who has been tempted in every way, just as we are--yet was without sin."* Jesus was tempted in every way, JUST AS WE ARE. But He won the war—for us! Jesus always remembered that Satan was prowling, and He crushed the dragon so we would not be crushed by him.

In total, sixteen of Satan's lies have been exposed in this book. To recap, they are:

Satan's Lies

- I don't exist

- Life is all luck and coincidence

- Life is supposed to get easier

- Some people are beyond God's grace

- What you do doesn't really matter

- You need more than what you've got

- A Christian never feels afraid

- You have all the time in the world

- I'm in control

- If Jesus was your savior, he'd do more for you

- You have to get caught up

- You should really keep your mouth shut

- You shouldn't bother God with your problems

- You're better off on your own

- You really can't change who you are

- You can forget about me now

That's a lot to remember. And, unfortunately, there are many more lies Satan will toss into your life. That's why, in this parting chapter, I want to give you four basic strategies from God's Word that will help you live in Christ's victory over Satan. These are four things you can do so you won't forget the battle that is raging, so Satan's lies won't dominate your life even after you close this book.

Strategy 1 – Be self-controlled and alert

1 Peter 5:8 says, *"Be self-controlled and alert. Your enemy the devil prowls around like a roaring lion looking for someone to devour."* This verse is not asking you to get tough in life. It's asking you to get the Spirit of God in your life. Remember, self-control is a fruit of the Holy Spirit (Galatians 5:22-23). The fruit of the Spirit are not qualities you earn or conjure up in your life. They are gifts. They are gifts given by the Spirit. How do you keep the Spirit in your life? One way is constant contact with God's Word. Ephesians 1:13 says, *"And you also were included in Christ when you heard the word of truth, the gospel of your salvation. Having believed, you were marked in him with a seal, the promised Holy Spirit."* God's Word and the Holy Spirit go together. The Holy Spirit testifies to what Jesus said. He brings us the truth of Christ (John 14:26). In order to have self-control, you need to be hearing and reading the Bible.

You may think, "The Bible? I can't read that! It's boring. I can't understand it." My response is: it's time to work at reading it. Get a translation you can understand. Read a verse each day. But don't neglect God's Word in your life!

Think about what's coming into your life now: TV images of sexual irresponsibility, violence, disrespect, and murder; questions about truth and life; difficult issues and problems. How will you be alert and self-controlled when everything in life is wearing down your senses and weakening your spirit? Your key to being alert to Satan's attacks and being self-controlled under temptation is being rooted in God's Word of life.

Strategy 2 – Cast Your Cares

1 Peter 5:7 says, *"Cast all your anxiety on him because he cares for you."* This strategy means prayer. Do you pray? I'm not talking about saying grace before meals or reciting a bedtime prayer with your kids. I'm talking about developing the discipline of constant dialog with God. The writings and comments of a man called Brother Lawrence were compiled into a little book called <u>Practicing the Presence of God</u>. His emphasis was to develop an ongoing conversation with God. He said,

> "Devoting yourself entirely to prayer would be the best thing you could do for yourself. God does not ask much of you. But remembering Him, praising Him, asking for His grace, offering Him your troubles, or thanking Him for what He has given you will console you all the time. During your meals or during any daily duty, lift your

heart up to Him, because even the least little remembrance will please Him. You don't have to pray out loud; He's nearer than you can imagine. It isn't necessary that we stay in church in order to remain in God's presence. We can make our hearts personal chapels where we can enter anytime to talk to God privately. These conversations can be so loving and gentle, and anyone can have them."[1]

Notice that Paul even emphasized prayer as a key weapon of spiritual warfare: *"And pray in the Spirit on all occasions with all kinds of prayers and requests. With this in mind, be alert and always keep on praying for all the saints. Pray also for me, that whenever I open my mouth, words may be given me so that I will fearlessly make known the mystery of the gospel, for which I am an ambassador in chains. Pray that I may declare it fearlessly, as I should" (Ephesians 6:18-20).* These three verses sum up the "spiritual armor" section of Paul's writing in Ephesians 6. Paul mentions prayer four times! He says, "Always keep on praying"! Your ongoing dialog with God is critically important to your spiritual survival.

In order to be ready for each day's battle after you close this book and put it on a shelf, it is important for you to grow as a person who prays continually (1 Thessalonians 5:17). Constant conversation with God means He is always in the picture. You're not driving Him away. You're inviting Him to stay close—exactly where He wants to be. As Brother Lawrence said, prayer is not just for church. It is an intimate dialog with your Savior God who gladly takes your burdens and who tenaciously guards your every step.

Strategy 3 – Resist and Stand Firm

1 Peter 5:9 says, *"Resist him, standing firm in the faith, because you know that your brothers throughout the world are undergoing the same kind of sufferings."* Here Peter lifts up community. You can resist and stand firm because you know you are not alone in your suffering. Everyone else out there isn't running wild and having a party. Everyone else isn't enjoying smooth sailing. No, you have brothers and sisters in the faith who are going through the same thing you are.

Sometimes you feel like you're the only person who is struggling. God knew that would happen. Remember, He is the one who reveals Satan's schemes. So, God's proactive answer to isolation was the church. The church was designed to be God's support mechanism for the believer. It was designed to be a place of refuge, a place of growth, a place of rest, a place to be loved, a place to use your gifts, a place to give and serve, and a place to be refilled. The church was designed to be a living and breathing manifestation of the presence of Christ.

Are you thinking, "My church isn't that way!"? Maybe not. Churches struggle with conflict, priorities, and keeping things relevant. Churches are not perfect. But the God-established reasons for the church, and your participation in a church community, are critical for your spiritual survival! One reason the church has so many problems is because it is a primary target of Satan. Of course he's going to try to make it awful! Of course he's going to try to turn you off to it! Of course he's going to do his all to eliminate it from your life! But I ask you: will you let him? Or will you relentlessly pursue the community of faith? Will you receive the blessings of fellowship God gives? Will you contribute to the strength of the whole as you participate in the body?

You'll be able to resist and stand firm as long as you are together with fellow believers.

Strategy 4 – Live in God's Strength and Promise

Again we hear from Peter: *"And the God of all grace, who called you to his eternal glory in Christ, after you have suffered a little while, will himself restore you and make you strong, firm and steadfast" (1 Peter 5:10).* Peter witnessed this personally. After his denial and failure, Jesus graciously restored him. Peter was a living example of God's strength and promise.

That's the only way you and I can make it through the darkness of this age. When all looks lost, we have the strength of Christ and the promise of His coming. And this is not merely positive thinking from God. When you are baptized into Christ you receive the Holy Spirit. You are filled with God's strength. When you eat the bread and wine of communion, you are filled with the presence of Jesus—the promise of His coming is true. He is with you and will be coming again.

God does not give us imaginary stories to keep our minds occupied while Satan rages. He gives us Himself, His presence. We have the promise that one day the battles will be over. One day the victory proclamation will be heard by all in heaven and on earth and under the earth. One day all will bow at the name of Jesus (Philippians 2:10).

The only way I have been able to make it to this point in my life is through God's strength and promise. That's also the only way I can face the future. If you take a hard and realistic look at life, it is much too great a burden for anyone. Whether it is living in blessing or difficulty, we're easy targets for Satan. The only way to make it through life is with the God of all grace. And isn't it amazing that He called us to do life with Him?

That's a perfect ending for this book and a perfect beginning for your life as you face tomorrow. And when that great day comes when we are all together before the throne of the Lamb, I look forward to seeing you. Just think, on that day, what the devil said will finally be true: we will be able to forget about him. No lie.

Notes for Chapter 16
[1] Brother Lawrence. <u>Practicing the Presence of God.</u> New Kensington, Pennsylvania: Whitaker House, 1982, 37.

Satan's Lies
Overcoming the Devil's attempts to Stunt Your Spiritual Growth

Reality Check
Study Guide

Reality Check – Lie #1: I Don't Really Exist

Read Revelation chapter 12.

What new things do you learn from this chapter about:

- The struggle between God and Satan

- The character of Satan

- The activity of Satan

- Where you stand between God and Satan

Review Ephesians 6:10-20

- How do you see the truth of these verses in your life today?

- Discuss how each weapon is being used or unused in your life. How can you grow in being clothed with a complete set of spiritual armor?

- How has this chapter helped reveal spiritual warfare in your life? What vulnerable points do you have for Satan's attacks?

- Discuss how Jesus gives you hope as you face the reality of spiritual warfare.

Reality Check – Lie #2: Life is All Luck and Coincidence

Read Psalm 139:1-16

- What do these verses say about how God is involved with your life?

- What does it mean for your day to day existence when you understand that your life is no accident?

- How does this word from God counteract the overwhelming feeling that life is a chaotic mess?

- How is your life in chaos these days?

- How does this word from God help you?

Read Ephesians 1:3-6

- What strategic position in God's Kingdom do these verses say you are in?

- What does it mean for your life's mission?

Read 2 Corinthians 5:17-20

- What is your mission according to these verses?

- How are you accomplishing that right now (at home and away from home)?

Read John 3:16

- Try to describe how much God loves you.

Read Galatians 2:20

- Why is this verse Good News for your life?

- How does this give you resources for each day?

Reality Check – Lie #3: Life is Supposed to Get Easier

Read John 16:33

- How do you and people in our culture expect life to get easier?

- What helps perpetuate this myth?

Read Luke 12:48

- How does this statement of Jesus speak to the increasing challenges of your life?

- How do you notice that life gets more difficult?

- What comfort is there in getting "behind Jesus"?

- What does it mean to be in that place?

- What areas of your life need to get in line behind Him better?

- How do the insights of this chapter help you approach your sacrifice and service for Christ in a better way?

- How does this chapter help you prepare for the future?

Reality Check – Lie #4: Some People Are Beyond God's Grace

Read John 9:1-3

- When do you find yourself making the assumption that someone is a lost cause?

- When do you feel like YOU are a lost cause?

- What did Jesus' answer tell the disciples about the blind man?

- What does Jesus' answer tell you about your life?

Read John 9:10-34

- What assumptions did the Pharisees have wrong?

- How does this impact the assumptions you make?

- How can your witness to God's grace in your life be like the witness of the healed blind man?

264

Read John 9:35-38

- How do Jesus' actions give you hope for His action in your life?

- How has Jesus shown His grace to you?

- How do you worship Him for that?

- Where do you need God's grace these days?

- What is God's response?

Reality Check – Lie #5: What You Do Doesn't Really Matter

Luke 10:1-20

- What has Jesus sent you to do at this time in your life?

- How do you feel about it?

- Look at verse 20. What did Jesus say was most important about your life?

- Contrast what the world says is most important with what you read in this chapter. How do you feel pressured to go the way of the world?

- Who has impacted you most in life? Explain how.

- Whom has God put in your life to impact? How are you doing it?

- How was Frank Harwood a hero?

- How are you fatigued in the assignment God has given you? What are some ways you can be sustained in your journey?

- What is the story (or stories) behind your story these days and forever?

Reality Check – Lie #6: You Need More Than What You've Got

Read Luke 16:19-31

- Think about times of suffering in your life. How have you felt that God wasn't doing enough?

- If you're looking back on suffering, what did God do to give His help, show His presence, and work His blessing?

- Think about times of prosperity. How were you tempted to think YOU were the one responsible for your blessing?

- If you are going through either prosperity or blessing right now, describe how God is working in your life.

- What is your ultimate need in life? What did God do about it? Describe how the rich man and how Lazarus viewed their ultimate need in life.

- Who in your life needs to hear about their ultimate need in life? Decide to talk with that person.

Read Psalm 119:33-176 (It could take a while! Keep notes.)

- Psalm 119 is all about God's Word. Words like "law," "precepts," and "decrees" refer to the Bible. Discuss what these verses about God's "love letter" tell you about God and yourself.

Reality Check – Lie #7: A Christian Never Feels Afraid

Read Romans 3:12-17

- These verses are a fierce description of the sin in this world. What makes you afraid as you go through life?

- Why is it important to take sin seriously? How do you overlook the true nature of a sinful world?

- How would you explain Martin Luther's balanced introduction to the explanation of the Ten Commandments: "We should fear and love God..."?

- How does the fear of God show itself in your life?

- What do you understand or not understand about the fear of God?

Read Matthew 13:18-23

- In this explanation to the parable of the sower, discuss the ways Jesus described that people fall away from Him.

- How do these ways affect your life?

- Whom do you know that has fallen away from Jesus or never has known Christ?

- How does healthy fear for their lives motivate you to reach them?

- Discuss healthy and unhealthy fear in the life of a believer.

Reality Check – Lie #8: You Have All the Time in the World

Read Luke 12:4-5

- Discuss Jesus' strong words that focus on getting your soul right.

- Is your soul right with God?

- Talk about how a person avoids the terror of hell, and, instead, can be assured of life with God in heaven.

- Have you ever had a life-threatening experience? Talk about it and how it can influence the way you look at the prospect of eternity.

Read Luke 12:13-15

- What does Jesus say about the importance of relationships?

- What is a primary obstacle to doing well in your relationships?

- How do you experience that in your life?

- Discuss what is really important in life. How does your life reflect that list of priorities?

Read Luke 12:16-21

- Are you doing well with what you have? Explain.

- How would you summarize the purpose God gives you for your life?

- What changes do you need to make in life to get closer to fulfilling this purpose?

- Is there anything that needs to be done in your life that you've been putting off?

- How can you guard yourself against Satan's lie that you have all the time in the world?

Reality Check – Lie #9: I'm in Control

Read Luke 22:31-35

- Discuss why God allows evil and suffering in life. Use insights from the chapter to guide your discussion.

- What "sifting" do you seem to be going through? How do you feel about it?

- Discuss how Jesus goes all out for you when you are suffering. Talk about Christ's intercession for you, the status of your faith, the outcome of your trial, and the purpose God may have in it.

- How has suffering in your life been used to bring you into honesty before God?

- What would you say to someone who claimed that the devil is in control of life?

- When do you panic in life? How does verse 35 help you?

Reality Check – Lie #10: If Jesus Was Your Savior, He'd Do More For You

Read Luke 23:35-43

- Why couldn't the people around the cross see who Jesus really was? What was standing in the way?

- How might your ideas of what Jesus should do in your life push the reality of Jesus out of your life?

- How does the devil try to convince you that Jesus should do more for you?

- Have you gone through the steps the second criminal took as he turned to Christ? Evaluate those steps and compare them to your life.

- What is comforting for you about Jesus' words in verse 43?

Read Psalm 25:7

- Discuss how the Lord remembers you. Talk about both options presented in this verse and why the Lord's way is a relief.

- Watch for Jesus over the next few days. Note what you see. Discuss it with a group of Christian friends.

Reality Check – Lie #11: You Have to Get Caught Up

Do the life-evaluation exercise at the end of the chapter, then discuss the questions below:

- What did you discover as you evaluated your annual, monthly, weekly and daily rhythms of life?

- What changes do you need to make?

- What insights did you gain as you examined the long-term evaluation?

Read Mark 6:12-13, 30-31

- How do you find yourself believing Satan's lie that you have to get caught up?

- How is hurry dominating your life right now?

- How can God's help be a bigger part of your life?

- Discuss how making changes in your life and getting regular strength from God can help you feel more at peace with your pace.

- How do Jesus' words in verse 31 affect you today? What is He asking you to do?

Reality Check – Lie #12: You Should Really Keep Your Mouth Shut

Read Luke 19:39-40

- What did Jesus mean when He responded to the Pharisees?

Read Psalm 121

- Talk about a time in your life when you saw God help you. What leads you to say "Help!" these days?

Read 1 John 1:9

- Think about the sins you need to confess to God. Silently do that in this study time.

- How can you practice saying "I'm sorry. I was wrong" in your life? To whom do you need to say this more frequently?

Read 1 John 4:10-17

- How did God show His love to you?

- How can you show love better to the people God has placed in your life?

- To whom do you need to say "I love you" these days?

Read 1 Peter 3:15

- How would you express the hope you have in Jesus?

- When is the last time you discussed that with the people close to you?

- How can you be better prepared to say "May I tell you?" in key situations in your life?

Reality Check – Lie #13: You Shouldn't Bother God with Your Problems

Read Matthew 15:21-28

- Jesus was very clear about God's specific plan. Why is that a comfort in your life? How can it cause you stress?

- How do these verses communicate the love of Jesus?

- How have you seen the love of God demonstrated in your life?

- Discuss the comments in this chapter about the "image of God." What do you think? How does that deepen your understanding of God's mindset at creation?

- The chapter says that God is unchanging, but He changes. Discuss this point and how it relates to your interaction with God.

- How is it a comfort that God is your listener?

- How has God grown your faith lately as you have interacted with Him?

- Do you wrestle with God? What are some big issues you've been presenting to God? Has He given you any blessings or any response?

- Discuss the three ways God helps you. Are you satisfied with His help?

- What obstacles does Satan put in your way when it comes to bringing your problems to God?

Reality Check – Lie #14: You're Better Off On Your Own

Read Luke 9:49-50

- When do you tend to try to make it on your own? Whom do you alienate in the process?

- Do you struggle with pride? How does that struggle affect forming and maintaining relationships in your life?

- How does Jesus direct John in this reading? What message was Jesus giving about the future of John's work? How did it impact John (think about the letters he wrote at the end of the Bible)?

Read 1 Corinthians 12:12-27

- Discuss how the church is designed to work. How do you feel about this design?

- What goes wrong in churches to foul up this design of God? What sins are at the root of the problems?

- How can you help your church fulfill God's plan?

- How can you grow in depending on the body of Christ instead of just yourself?

Reality Check – Lie #15: You Can't Really Change Who You Are

Read John 3:1-17

- Notice that Nicodemus came to Jesus at night. There was fear in his life. What fears do you have about your life?

- How do you feel chained to the past?

- What experiences in your life leave you feeling hopeless about the future?

- Why was John in the story so resistant to Nels' approaches? What is at the root of your resistance to God's help?

- What spiritual warfare do you notice in your life—especially in areas of struggle for you? What is Satan doing? How is God fighting for you?

- What does Jesus mean in verses 5, 6, 7, and 8? How do His words apply to your life?

- How does your life need to be changed? List all the ways you can think of—big and small.

- How do verses 16-17 give you hope for change happening?

Reality Check – Lie #16: You Can Forget About Me Now

Read 1 Peter 5:7-10

- What is a critical component of being a person who is self-controlled and alert?

- How do you cast your anxiety on the Lord? Evaluate your discipline of conversing with God.

- Discuss the value of gathering together as a church. What are some pros and cons about church? How can you help to make church a better experience?

- How does God dwell in you with His strength? What are some ways you have seen Him present in your life? What hope does that give you?

- How might Satan lull you into forgetting about him in the days ahead?

- What are some specific ways you can stay aware of his schemes without getting preoccupied with his antics?

- What was the most helpful part of this book for your life? Discuss areas that especially addressed your needs. Discuss insights that you gained while reading the book.

- What top three follow-up actions can you implement so you can preserve and continue to build on the growth this book has given you?

Acknowledgements

A project like this requires the support of many people. I would like to thank my colleague in ministry, Scott Christenson, for his help in developing the themes for each of these chapters. This book started out as a sermon series. Scott and I enjoyed preaching on these subjects during the course of a ministry season. It was a joy to work with him.

I also give thanks to God for the people of Prince of Peace Lutheran Church. They allowed me some sabbatical time to write chapters and develop "Satan's Lies" into a book. Their support in ministry has been one of the greatest blessings in my life.

I owe a deep debt of gratitude to my daughters. During my time at home they gave me the freedom to write in my chilly basement study—even sharing the computer that was reserved for their homework! We enjoyed some breaks playing basketball and other fun activities as this book was put together.

For my wife, Cindy, words of thanks cannot ever completely express my deep gratitude for her support, love, faith, and inspiration. I could not do what I do without her. God has blessed me with her, my best friend.

Finally, I thank Jesus for walking with me, giving me words, and showing me He is in it for the long haul. Satan cannot outlast the Savior, my Savior! I hope He is yours, too.

Michael W. Newman

About the Author

Michael Newman has been a pastor, teacher, author, and speaker for over 20 years. He has served churches in Texas, Minnesota, and in the Chicago area, and continues to be active in writing, and in a variety of preaching and teaching venues. Married to his wife Cindy since 1983, they have been blessed with two wonderful daughters. When not preaching and teaching, you might catch him hanging out with his family, running a few miles on the Texas roads, risking his life doing yard work, or enjoying a good book.